영문법 판매 1위, 중학영문법 3800제의 초등시리즈

초등영문법 3800제

LEVEL 2

입문 2단계

발행 초판 19쇄(2024년 8월 29일)

책임편집 서은숙 **편집** 성은혜 **원고집필** 정다혜, 권은정, 김주현, 정은주, 김유미, 홍주희 **연습문제집필** 조윤경, 권은정, 김송이, 김주희

워크북집필 윤정한, 정다혜, 김주희, 김송이 **원고검토** 유예슬, 최희찬, 박문정, 백경빈, 김미경, 김규은, 양원석, 고민정 **영문감수** Kathryn O'Handley

감수 오현진(강남구청 중등인강 강사) **교정** 황희진, 정다혜, 김주희, 이은영, 하은옥, 홍성경, 오정훈, 심가원, 이은혜, 신영은, 김송이, 하새롬

베타테스트 신재진, 이옥현, 유윤정, 정요한, 신소미, 장신혜, 변선영, 정은주

녹음 와이알 미디어 **녹음대본정리** 신소미, 김소정, 김건탁, 김윤아, 최안나 **녹음검수** 이상미, 신소미, 김소정, 김주희, 윤수경, 이옥현, 이유진, 최안나

사진검색 신의진, 김윤아, 이은혜, 손주연 **삽화** 박현주 **표지디자인** 김연실 **인디자인편집** 정은영, 박정민, 박경아, 김미라, 고연화

제작 이주영 **발행처** ㈜마더텅 **발행인** 문숙영 **주소** 서울시 금천구 가마산로 96, 708호

초등영문법 3800제 입문 2단계

이렇게 공부하세요.

LEVEL 2

STEP 1

문법 개념을 익힌 후 확인테스트를 풀어보면서 제대로 이해했는지 확인해요.

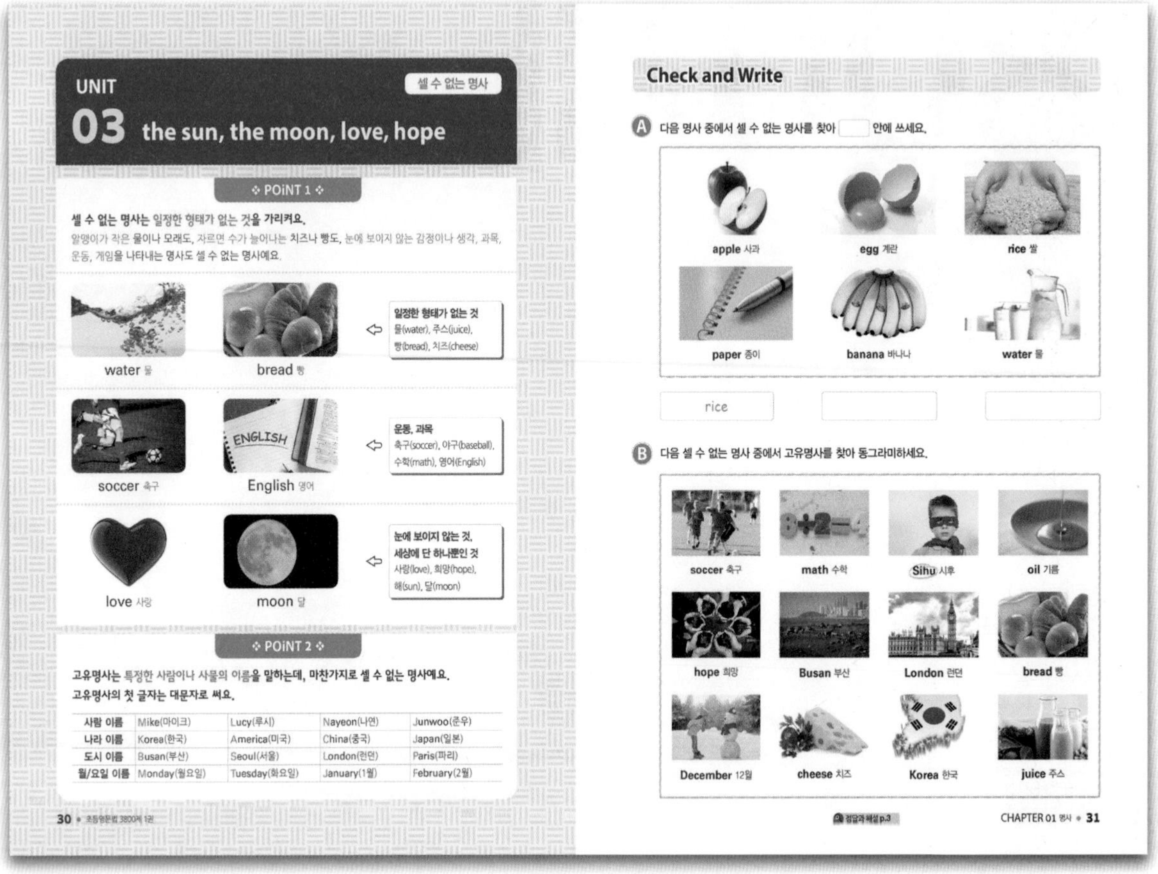

STEP 2

Practice 1, 2, 3

Practice 1, 2, 3로 구성된 연습문제를 풀면서 앞에서 배운 문법이 적용된 풍부한 예문을 접할 수 있어요. 연습 문제들을 풀다보면, 서술형 문제도 더 이상 어렵지 않아요!

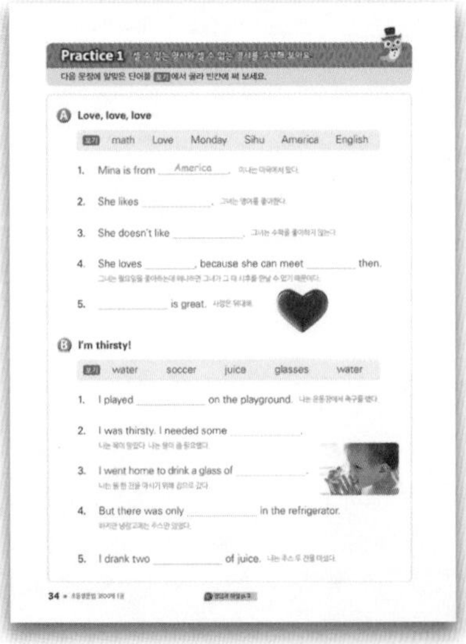

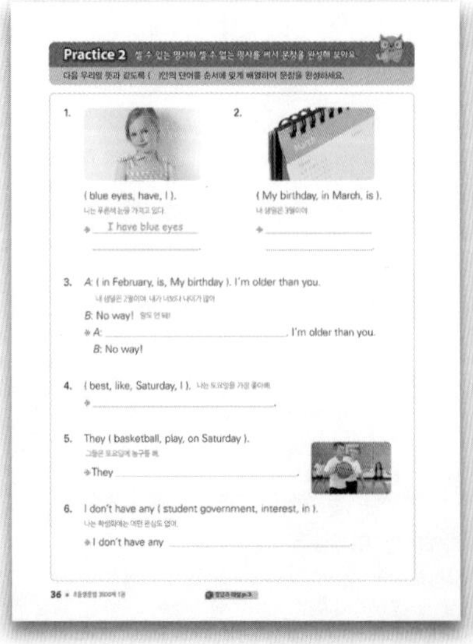

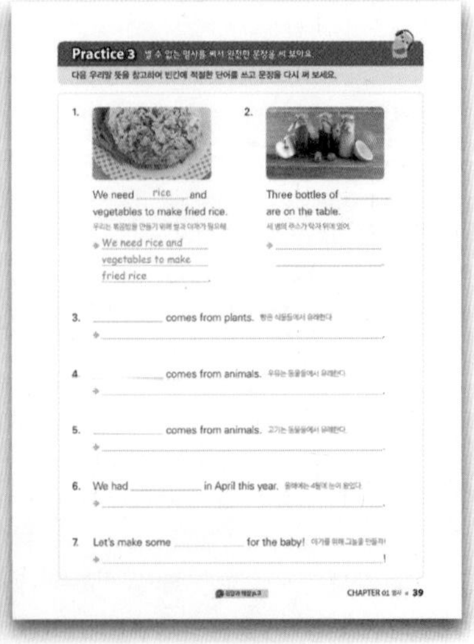

STEP 3

Let's Practice More!

문법 내용을 제대로 이해했는지 확인할 수 있도록 SET 01~08까지 다양한 유형의 연습문제를 실었어요.
문제를 하나하나 풀다보면 해당 UNIT의 핵심 개념을 제대로 익히게 될 거에요.

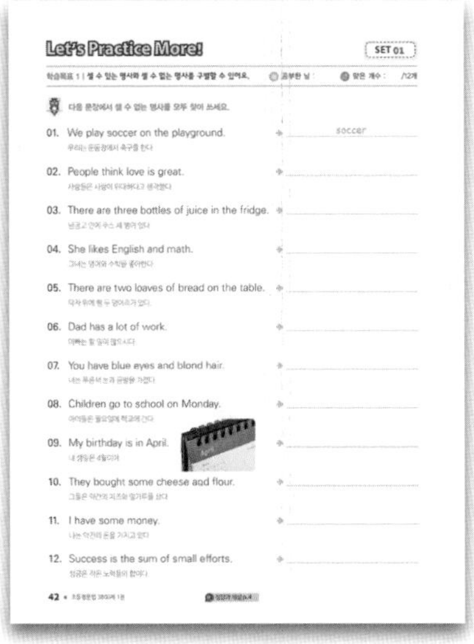

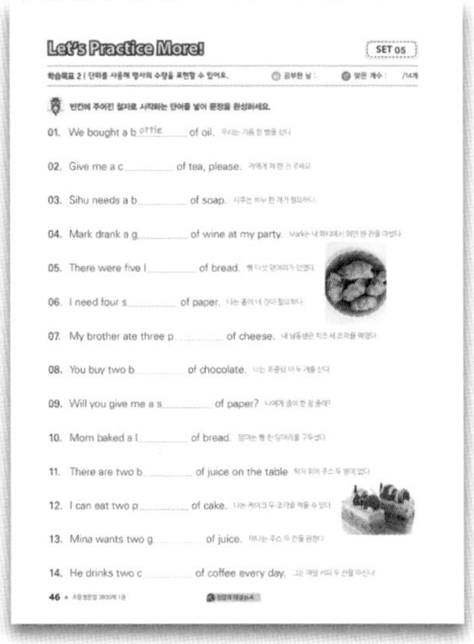

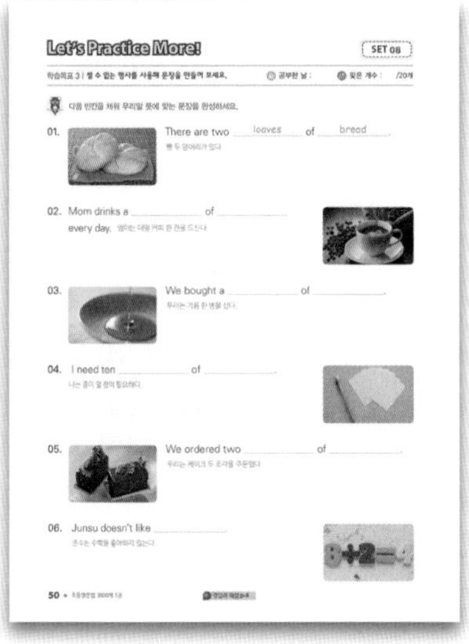

STEP 4

마무리 실전테스트

최종 마무리 테스트로서 권당 2회분의 실전테스트를 실었어요. 총 30문제의 진단평가 및 교내평가 유형의 실전문제로 앞에서 배운 내용을 복습하고 취약한 부분을 파악해 봐요.

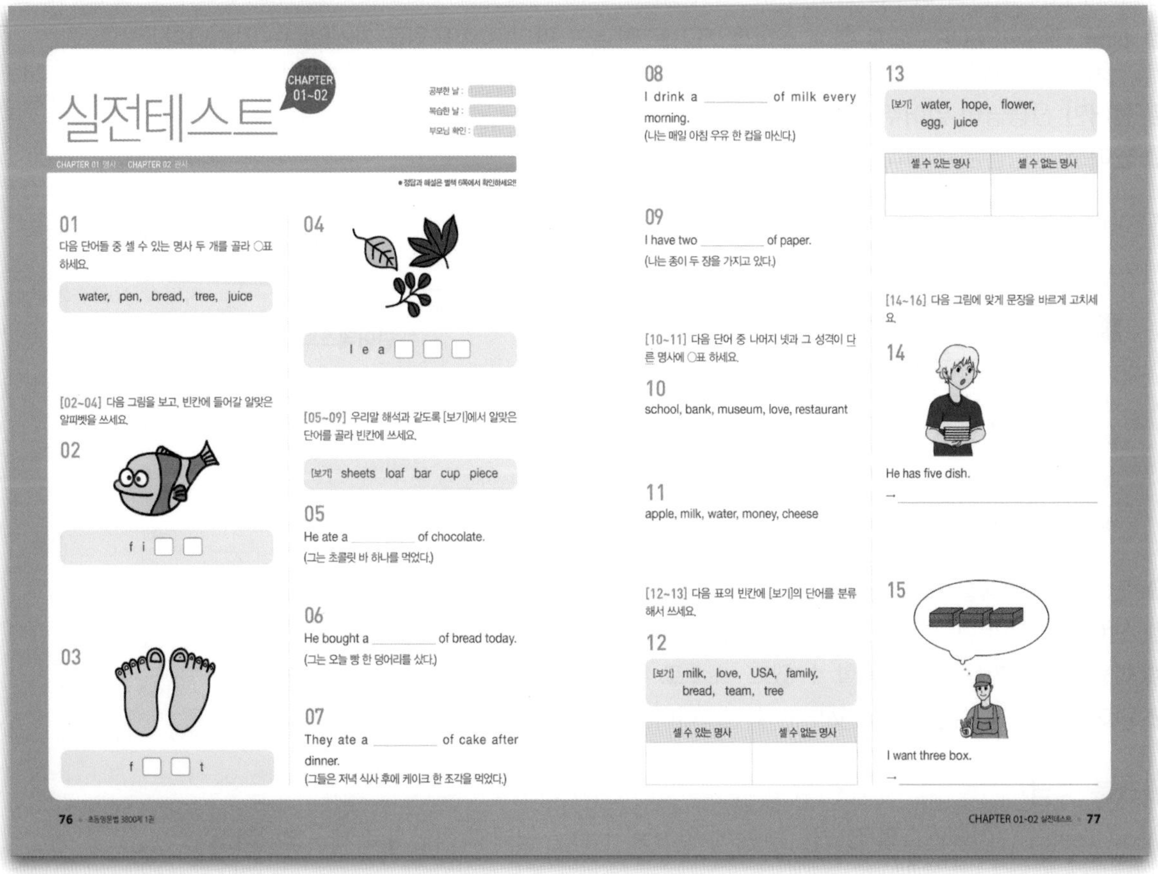

워크북 구성 및 활용법 워크북은 아래와 같은 방법으로 활용하세요.

1. 단어쓰기 연습

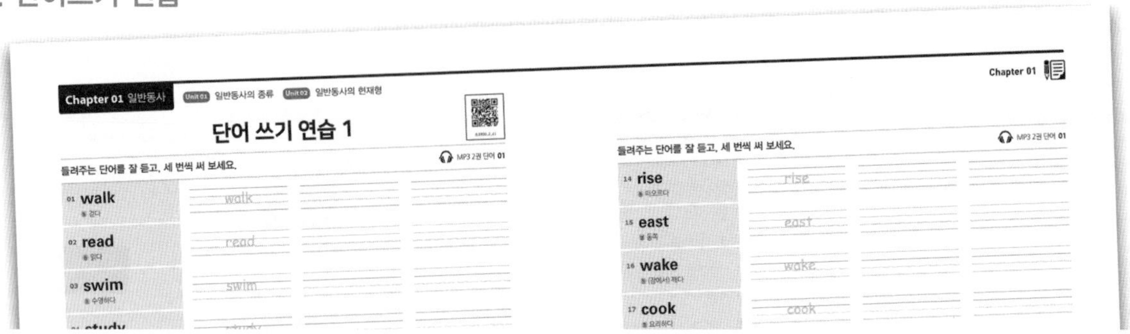

❶ 먼저 본문 학습을 마무리 합니다.
❷ 해당 페이지의 QR코드를 통해 스마트 기기로 빠르고 편리하게 음원을 재생할 수 있습니다. 전체 음원 파일은 마더텅 홈페이지(www.toptutor.co.kr)에서 다운로드 가능합니다.
❸ 원어민 선생님이 읽어주는 영단어를 잘 듣고 안내선 안에 영어 단어 철자를 세 번씩 쓰세요.

2. 받아쓰기 시험 (Dictation Test)

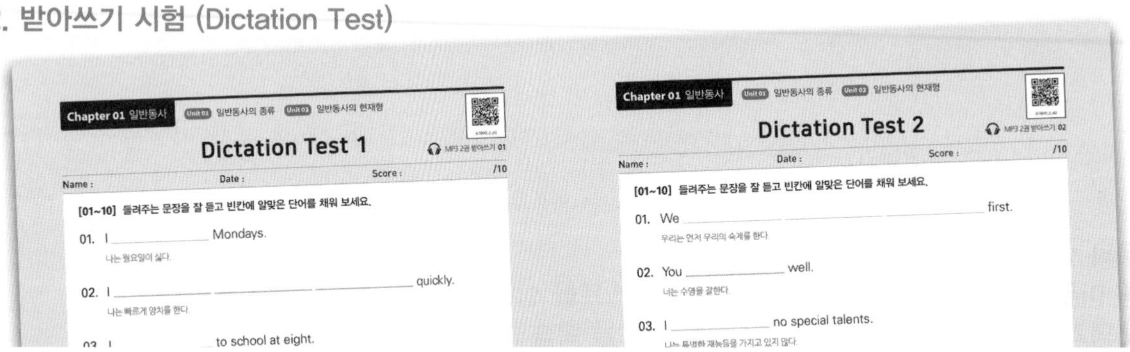

❶ 먼저 본문 학습을 마무리 합니다.
❷ 해당 페이지의 QR코드를 통해 스마트 기기로 빠르고 편리하게 음원을 재생할 수 있습니다. 전체 음원 파일은 마더텅 홈페이지(www.toptutor.co.kr)에서 다운로드 가능합니다.
❸ 원어민 선생님이 읽어주는 문장을 잘 듣고, 빈칸을 채우세요.
❹ 받아쓰기 정답은 워크북 뒷부분에 있습니다.

3. 단어테스트

❶ 단어쓰기 연습을 하며, 단어들을 암기합니다.
❷ 단어테스트의 한글 뜻을 보고 암기한 영단어를 써 보세요.
❸ 학원에서 평가용으로 활용할 수 있고, 스스로 확인하는 용도로 활용할 수도 있습니다.
❹ 단어테스트 정답은 워크북 뒷부분에 있습니다.

4. 워크북 정답

Dictation Test와 단어테스트의 정답을 한 눈에 알아보기 쉬운 형태의 정답지로 제공합니다.

영문법 판매 1위, 중학영문법 3800제의 초등시리즈

초등영문법 3800제

2 LEVEL

입문 2단계 CONTENTS

Chapter 01 일반동사

이 챕터에서는 움직임이나 감정, 생각을 나타내는 '동사'에 대해 익히고,
동사의 형태 변화에 대해 배워 보아요.

☆ 학습 방향 및 배울 내용 미리보기 ☆

- ☐ **Unit 01 : I like** pizza.
  일반동사의 종류
  움직임이나 감정, 생각을 나타내는 대표적인 일반동사들을 알려 줄게요.

▼

- ☐ **Unit 02 :** You **have** a pet.
  일반동사의 현재형
  일반동사의 현재형은 어떤 때 쓰고, 어떤 형태인지 배워 보아요.

▼

- ☐ **Unit 03 :** My mother **works** at the school.
  일반동사의 3인칭 단수형 (1)
  주어가 3인칭 단수일 때 일반동사의 형태가 어떻게 변하는지 알아보아요.

▼

- ☐ **Unit 04 :** My sister **studies** hard.
  일반동사의 3인칭 단수형 (2)
  주어가 3인칭 단수일 때 일반동사의 형태가 불규칙적으로 변하는 경우에 대해 알아보아요.

단어 미리보기

이 챕터에 나올 단어들 중 이미 알고 있는 단어가 있나요?
맞는 뜻을 골라 체크해 봐요.

날짜 : 　　　이름 : 　　　알고 있는 단어의 수 : 　　　/24개

No.	아는 단어	단어	품사	알맞은 뜻에 체크 표시해 봐요.			
1	✔	walk	동사	걷다	✔	달리다	☐
2	☐	read	동사	쓰다	☐	읽다	☐
3	☐	swim	동사	수영하다	☐	흔들다	☐
4	☐	study	동사	공부하다	☐	놀다	☐
5	☐	hate	동사	싫어하다	☐	좋아하다	☐
6	☐	want	동사	사다	☐	원하다	☐
7	☐	wish	동사	바라다	☐	축하하다	☐
8	☐	know	동사	모르다	☐	알다	☐
9	☐	think	동사	생각하다	☐	찾다	☐
10	☐	doll	명사	친구	☐	인형	☐
11	☐	family	명사	할머니	☐	가족	☐
12	☐	weekend	명사	주말	☐	주중	☐
13	☐	work	동사	일하다	☐	운전하다	☐
14	☐	say	동사	말하다	☐	수줍어하다	☐
15	☐	prepare	동사	준비하다	☐	공격하다	☐
16	☐	eat	동사	먹다	☐	마시다	☐
17	☐	run	동사	달리다	☐	걷다	☐
18	☐	fast	부사	천천히	☐	빨리	☐
19	☐	drive	동사	운전하다	☐	잠수하다	☐
20	☐	office	명사	사무실	☐	놀이터	☐
21	☐	always	부사	항상	☐	가끔	☐
22	☐	pass	동사	실패하다	☐	통과하다	☐
23	☐	exam	명사	공책	☐	시험	☐
24	☐	finish	동사	끝내다	☐	시작하다	☐

UNIT 01 I like pizza.

일반동사의 종류

일반동사는 움직임을 나타내는 동사, 감정 · 생각을 나타내는 동사로 나뉘어요!

❖ POiNT 1 ❖

행동을 나타내는 일반동사 움직임을 나타내요!

walk 걷다

eat 먹다

read 읽다

play 놀다

swim 수영하다

study 공부하다

❖ POiNT 2 ❖

상태를 나타내는 일반동사 감정이나 생각을 나타내요!

like 좋아하다

hate 싫어하다

want 원하다

wish 바라다

know 알다

think 생각하다

Check and Write

다음 문장을 읽고 일반동사를 찾아 빈칸에 쓰세요.

1. I have a pair of cute socks.
나는 귀여운 양말 한 켤레를 가지고 있어.
have

2. I want a computer for Christmas.
나는 크리스마스에 컴퓨터를 원해요.

3. We play soccer on Saturdays.
우리는 토요일마다 축구를 해.

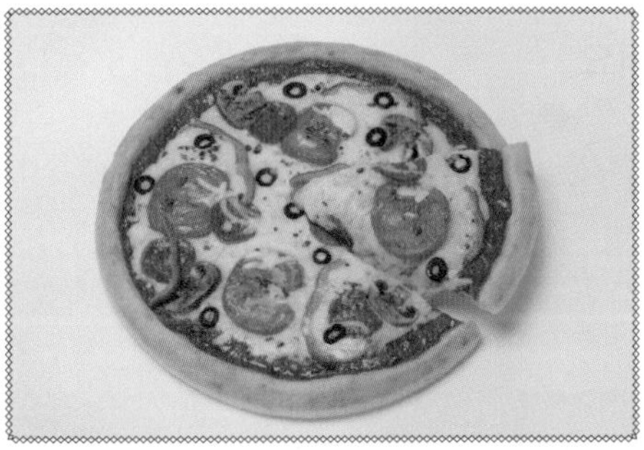

4. I like pizza.
나는 피자를 좋아해.

5. We go to school at 8:30.
우리는 8시 30분에 학교에 가.

정답과 해설 p.2

UNIT 02 You have a pet.

일반동사의 현재형

❖ POiNT 1 ❖

일반동사의 현재형은 현재 일어나고 있는 사실을 말하기 위한 표현이에요.

주어가 3인칭 단수일 경우에는 동사원형에 -s를 붙이고, 그 외의 경우에는 모두 동사원형 그대로 써요!

I/we/you/they	play
	have
he/she/it	plays
	has

I play Cookie Run on Sundays.
나는 일요일마다 쿠키런을 해.

You have a pet.
너는 애완동물을 갖고 있어.

He plays the computer games every day.
그는 매일 컴퓨터 게임을 해.

She *has many dolls. 그녀는 많은 인형들을 가지고 있어.

＊**대표적인 예외 have**
have의 3인칭 단수형은 has예요.
이렇게 불규칙한 일반동사의 현재형은 다음 단원에서 더 자세히 배워보기로 해요!

❖ POiNT 2 ❖

현재 시제의 쓰임

'지금' 일어나고 있는 일이 아니어도, 다음과 같은 경우에는 현재시제를 써요.

반복적으로 일어나는 일

Our family goes to the movies every weekend.
우리 가족은 주말마다 영화를 보러 가.

일반적인 사실

Americans speak English.
미국인들은 영어를 써.

변하지 않는 사실

The sun rises in the east.
해는 동쪽에서 떠.

Check and Write

다음 나열된 동사들 중 적절한 것을 골라 빈칸을 채워 보세요.

보기 wakes up play eat cook have live

1. We [play] basketball after school.
우리는 방과 후에 농구를 해.

2. I [ ] many Russian dolls.
나는 많은 러시아 인형을 가지고 있어.

3. He [ ] early in the morning.
그는 아침에 일찍 일어나.

4. I [ ] very well.
나는 요리를 아주 잘 해.

5. They [ ] next door.
그들은 옆집에 살아.

6. You [ ] chocolate too much.
너 초콜릿을 너무 많이 먹어.

정답과 해설 p.2

Practice 1 연습문제를 풀면서 상황에 맞는 적절한 일반동사를 익혀 보아요.

다음 문장에 알맞은 동사를 보기 에서 골라 빈칸에 써 보세요.

A Sihu's Monday morning

보기 eat get up hate put on brush walk

1. I ___hate___ Mondays.
   나는 월요일이 싫다.

2. I ___________at seven on Mondays.
   나는 월요일에 7시에 일어난다.

3. I ___________ my glasses right away. 나는 곧장 안경을 쓴다.

4. I ___________ breakfast with my family. 나는 가족과 함께 아침을 먹는다.

5. I ___________ my teeth quickly. 나는 빠르게 양치를 한다.

6. I ___________ to school at eight. 나는 8시에 걸어서 학교에 간다.

B Mina's weekend

보기 likes has stays up wakes listens sleeps

1. Mina ___________ weekends. 미나는 주말을 좋아한다.

2. She ___________ late at night. 그녀는 밤에 늦게까지 깨어있다.

3. She ___________ to Exo's music.
   그녀는 엑소의 음악을 듣는다.

4. She ___________ until 14:00 on weekends.
   그녀는 주말에 오후 2시까지 잔다.

5. She ___________ sweet dreams every night. 그녀는 매일 좋은 꿈을 꾼다.

6. Mom ___________ her up. 엄마가 그녀를 깨운다.

정답과 해설 p.2

C We want a vacation!

보기 go wake up hate want sleep

1. Many kids __________ early on Sundays to watch cartoons.
   많은 아이들은 만화를 보려고 일요일에 일찍 깬다.

2. But I __________ until 2:00 in the afternoon on Sundays.
   하지만 나는 일요일 오후 2시까지 잔다.

3. We __________ to bed early because tomorrow is Monday.
   내일은 월요일이기 때문에 우리는 일찍 잠자리에 든다.

4. That's why we __________ Mondays.
   그게 우리가 월요일을 싫어하는 이유다.

5. We __________ a vacation! 우린 방학을 원해!

D English test

보기 have study keep

1. I __________ hard. 나는 공부를 열심히 해.

2. I __________ an English test next Monday.
   나는 다음 주 월요일에 영어시험을 치거든.

3. I __________ my fingers crossed. 내가 행운을 빌게.

정답과 해설 p.2

Practice 2 일반동사를 써서 문장을 완성해 보아요.

다음 우리말 뜻과 같도록 주어진 표현을 순서에 맞게 배열하여 문장을 완성하세요.

1. (study hard, You).

너는 공부를 열심히 하는구나.

➔ You study hard ______________________________.

2. (my fingers crossed, I, keep).

내가 행운을 빌게.

➔ ______________________________ ______________________________.

3. (He, his homework, does) after school. 그는 방과 후에 숙제를 해.

➔ ______________________________ after school.

4. (I, video games, play) after school.

나는 방과 후에 비디오게임을 해.

➔ ______________________________ after school.

5. (an English test, I, have) next Monday.

난 다음 주 월요일에 영어시험을 쳐.

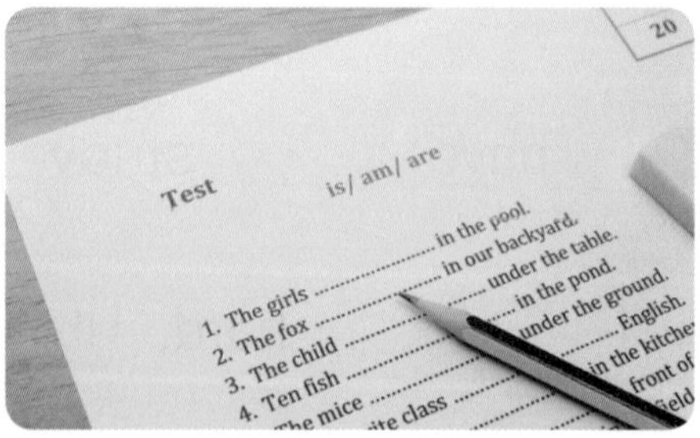

➔ ______________________________ next Monday.

6. (play, I, soccer) with my friends. 나는 친구들과 축구를 한다.

➔ ______________________________ with my friends.

정답과 해설 p.2

7. (I, the flu, have). (*flu : 독감) 나 독감 걸렸어.

➔ ______________________________.

8. (a runny nose, I, have). (*runny nose : 콧물) 나 콧물 나와.

➔ ______________________________.

9. (shots, I, hate)! 나는 주사가 싫어!

➔ ______________________________!

10. Mom, (have, I, a fever).
엄마, 나 열나요.

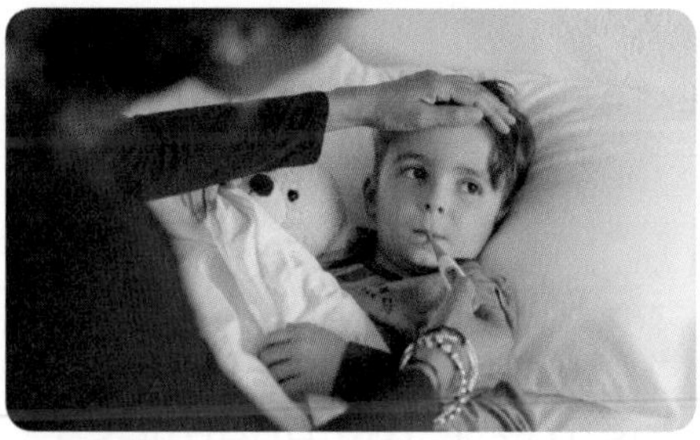

➔ Mom, ______________
______________.

11. (nags, She, me).
그녀는 나에게 잔소리를 해. (*nag: ~에게 잔소리하다)

➔ ______________
______________.

12. ("Crayon Shin-chan", watch, I). 나는 '짱구는 못 말려'를 봐.

➔ ______________________________.

13. (use, your smartphone, You) too much. 넌 스마트폰을 너무 많이 써.

➔ ______________________ too much.

14. (fall down, and get up again, They). 그들은 넘어지고 다시 일어나는 거야.

➔ ______________________________.

정답과 해설 p.2

15. (like, I, warm hugs).

난 따뜻한 포옹을 좋아해.

→ ______________________________

______________________________.

16. (read, many books, We).

우리는 책을 많이 읽어.

→ ______________________________

______________________________.

17. (eat, ice cream, They). 그들은 아이스크림을 먹는다.

→ ____.

18. (die hard, habits, Old). 오래된 습관은 고치기 어렵다. (세 살 버릇 여든까지 간다.)

→ ____.

19. (have, I, no special talents).
I am passionately curious.

나는 특별한 재능들을 가지고 있지 않다.
나는 열렬히 호기심이 많을 뿐이다.

(*passionately : 열렬히)

*Albert Einstein

→ ______________________________

______________________________.

I am passionately curious.

20. (destroy, I, my enemies)
when I make them my friends.

내가 그들을 나의 친구로 만들 때,
나는 나의 적들을 없앤다.

(*destroy : 파괴하다)

*Abraham Lincoln

→ ______________________________

____

when I make them my friends.

정답과 해설 p.2

Practice 3 일반동사를 써서 완전한 문장을 써 보아요.

우리말 뜻을 참고하여 다음 주어진 표현을 사용해 문장을 완성해 보세요.

1. (love, "Detective Conan") 그는 '명탐정 코난'을 아주 좋아해.

→ He loves "Detective Conan" ______.

2. (dislike, "Pororo") 나는 '뽀로로'를 싫어해.

→ ______.

3. (want, a bicycle)

저는 크리스마스에 자전거를 원해요!

→ ______ for Christmas!

4. (need, a break)

난 휴식이 필요해.

→ ______ ______.

5. (Many kids, watch, cartoons)

많은 아이들은 일요일에 만화를 본다

→ ______ on Sundays.

6. (sleep, until 11 o'clock)

나는 주말에 11시까지 잔다.

→ ______ on weekends.

정답과 해설 p.2

7. (want, a "One Piece" figure) 저는 제 생일에 '원피스' 피규어를 원해요.

➔ ______________________________ for my birthday.

8. (watch, "Gag Concert") 나는 일요일에 '개그콘서트'를 본다.

➔ ______________________________.

9. (Most kids, go to bed, early) 대부분의 아이들은 일요일에 일찍 잔다.

➔ ______________________________.

10. (hate, Mondays) 나는 월요일이 싫어!

➔ ______________________________!

11. (hate, Mondays)

우리는 월요일을 싫어한다.

➔ ______________________________

______________________________.

12. (do, our homework)

우리는 우리의 숙제를 한다.

➔ ______________________________

______________________________.

13. (get up, late, in a hurry) 나는 늦게 일어나서 서둘러 학교에 간다.

➔ ______________________________.

14. (nag) (*nag : ~에게 잔소리하다) 나의 엄마는 나에게 잔소리를 하신다.

➔ ______________________________.

정답과 해설 p.2

15. (play, soccer)

그들은 방과 후에 축구를 해.

➔ ______________________________

after school.

16. (swim well)

너는 수영을 잘한다.

➔ ______________________________

______________________________.

17. (Mina, love) 미나가 너를 사랑해.

➔ ____.

18. (have, no, special talents)

나는 특별한 재능들을 가지고 있지 않다.

➔ ____.

19. (keep, at home)

나는 집에서 나의 스마트폰을 달고 산다.

➔ ______________________________

______________________________.

20. (like, Sihu)

나는 시후가 좋아.

➔ ______________________________

______________________________.

정답과 해설 p.2

Let's Practice More!

SET 01

학습목표 1 | **be동사와 일반동사를 구분해 보아요.** 공부한 날 : 맞은 개수 : /12개

다음 문장을 읽고 밑줄 친 동사가 바르게 쓰였으면 ○표, 틀리면 ×표를 하세요.

01. I hate Mondays. 난 월요일이 싫어. → ○

02. I am breakfast with my family. 난 가족들과 아침을 먹는다. → ________

03. She stays up late at night. 그녀는 밤늦게까지 깨어있어. → ________

04. She is to Exo's music. 그녀는 엑소의 음악을 듣는다. → ________

05. He has a nightmare. 그는 악몽을 꾼다. → ________

06. We are to bed early. 우리는 일찍 잠자리에 든다. → ________

07. I keep my fingers crossed. 내가 행운을 빌게. → ________

08. You do your homework after school. 너는 방과 후에 너의 숙제를 한다. → ________

09. I am no special talents. 난 특별한 재능들을 갖고 있지 않다. → ________

10. I am up late. 나는 늦게 일어난다. → ________

11. They play baseball after school. 그들은 방과 후에 야구를 한다. → ________

12. Mina likes you. 미나가 너를 좋아해. → ________

정답과 해설 p.2

Let's Practice More!

SET 02

학습목표 1 | **be동사와 일반동사를 구분해 보아요.** 공부한 날 : 맞은 개수 : /14개

다음 우리말 해석을 참고하여 알맞은 것을 고르세요.

01. I like Sihu. This (is / eats) a secret. 난 시후를 좋아해. 이건 비밀이야.

02. Americans (are / speak) English. 미국인들은 영어를 써.

03. I (am / have) a pair of cute socks. 난 귀여운 양말 한 켤레를 갖고 있어.

04. I (am / put on) my glasses. 난 내 안경을 쓴다.

05. They (are / make) cookies. 그것들은 쿠키이다.

06. They (are / study) hard these days. 그들은 요즘 공부를 열심히 해.

07. They (are / live) next door. 그들은 옆집에 살아.

08. Today (is / hates) Monday. 오늘은 월요일이다.

09. My aunt (is / likes) pizza. 나의 고모는 피자를 좋아하셔.

10. I (am / brush) my teeth quickly. 난 이를 빨리 닦는다.

11. Mina (is / likes) weekends. 미나는 주말을 좋아한다.

12. We (are / want) a vacation! 우리는 방학을 원해!

13. They (are / have) an English test next Monday. 그들은 다음 주 월요일에 영어시험을 봐.

14. My uncle (is / likes) a teacher. 나의 삼촌은 선생님이다.

정답과 해설 p.2

Let's Practice More!

SET 03

학습목표 1 | **be동사와 일반동사를 구분해 보아요.**　　공부한 날 :　　맞은 개수 :　　/14개

다음 우리말 해석을 읽고 빈칸에 알맞은 단어를 써 보세요.

01. 그녀는 매일 밤 좋은 꿈을 꾼다. ➔ She ___has___ sweet dreams every night.

02. 엄마가 그녀를 깨우셔. ➔ Mom ________ her up.

03. 난 영어를 아주 잘 해. ➔ I ________ English very well.

04. 그것들은 컴퓨터 게임이다. ➔ They ________ computer games.

05. 난 콧물이 나. ➔ I ________ a runny nose.

06. 엄마, 나 열나요. ➔ Mom, I ________ a fever.

07. 이것은 '짱구는 못 말려'이다. ➔ This ________ "Crayon Shin-chan."

08. 나는 영어를 가르친다. ➔ I ________ English.

09. 오래된 습관은 고치기 어렵다. (세 살 버릇 여든까지 간다.)
➔ Old habits ________ hard.

10. 이것은 '뽀로로'이다. ➔ This ________ "Pororo."

11. 난 크리스마스에 자전거를 원해요. ➔ I ________ a bicycle for Christmas.

12. 우리는 숙제를 먼저 한다. ➔ We ________ our homework first.

13. 너는 초콜릿을 너무 많이 먹어.
➔ You ________ chocolate too much.

14. 나의 삼촌은 피자를 좋아하셔. ➔ My uncle ________ pizza.

정답과 해설 p.2

Let's Practice More!

SET 04

학습목표 2 | 주어에 따라 달라지는 일반동사를 연습해 보아요. 공부한 날 : 맞은 개수 : /14개

밑줄 친 동사가 바르게 쓰였으면 ○표, 틀리면 ×표를 하세요.

01. I have a pair of cute socks. 난 귀여운 양말 한 켤레를 갖고 있어. → ○

02. I walks to school at eight. 난 8시에 걸어서 학교에 간다. → ______

03. I has a math test this Thursday. 나는 이번 주 목요일에 수학시험을 쳐. → ______

04. You use your smartphone too much. 넌 스마트폰을 너무 많이 써. → ______

05. We reads many books. 우리는 많은 책을 읽어. → ______

06. They eat ice cream. 그들은 아이스크림을 먹는다. → ______

07. The sun rises in the east. 태양은 동쪽에서 뜬다. → ______

08. I goes to school in a hurry. 난 서둘러 학교에 간다. → ______

09. You swim very well. 너는 수영을 아주 잘 한다. → ______

10. I keep my smartphone at home. 난 집에서 스마트폰을 달고 산다. → ______

11. Dad wake up early in the morning. 아빠는 아침에 일찍 일어나신다. → ______

12. I get up at seven. 난 7시에 일어나. → ______

13. I puts on my glasses. 난 내 안경을 쓴다. → ______

14. Mom wake her up. 엄마가 그녀를 깨우셔. → ______

정답과 해설 p.3

Let's Practice More!

SET 05

학습목표 2 | 주어에 따라 달라지는 일반동사를 연습해 보아요. 공부한 날 : 맞은 개수 : /12개

다음 문장을 읽고 ( ) 안에서 알맞은 것을 골라 보세요.

01. I (eat / eats) breakfast with my family. 난 가족들과 아침을 먹는다.

02. I (brush / brushes) my teeth quickly. 난 이를 빨리 닦는다.

03. She (stay / stays) up late at night.
그녀는 밤늦게까지 깨어 있어.

04. They (make / makes) cookies.
그들은 쿠키를 만든다.

05. He (have / has) a nightmare. 그는 악몽을 꾼다.

06. We (go / goes) to bed early. 우리는 일찍 잠자리에 든다.

07. I (keep / keeps) my fingers crossed. 내가 행운을 빌게.

08. They (live / lives) next door. 그들은 옆집에 살아.

09. You (use / uses) your smartphone too much. 넌 스마트폰을 너무 많이 써.

10. We (read / reads) many books.
우리는 책을 많이 읽어.

11. He (love / loves) "Detective Conan." 그는 '명탐정 코난'을 아주 좋아해.

12. I (need / needs) your help. 난 너의 도움이 필요해.

정답과 해설 p.3

Let's Practice More!

SET 06

학습목표 2 | 주어에 따라 달라지는 일반동사를 연습해 보아요. 공부한 날 : 맞은 개수 : /14개

다음 문장을 읽고 밑줄 친 부분을 올바르게 고쳐 보세요.

01. I has a pair of cute socks. → have
난 귀여운 양말 한 켤레를 갖고 있어.

02. Americans speaks English. → ______
미국인들은 영어를 써.

03. Dad wake up early in the morning. → ______
아빠는 아침에 일찍 일어나신다.

04. We goes to the movies every Saturday. → ______
우린 토요일마다 영화를 보러 가.

05. I keeps my smartphone at home. → ______
난 집에서 스마트폰을 달고 산다.

06. You swims very well. → ______
너는 수영을 아주 잘 한다.

07. I goes to school in a hurry. 난 서둘러 학교에 간다. → ______

08. I wants a "One Piece" figure for my birthday. → ______
저는 생일에 '원피스' 피규어를 원해요.

09. She have many dolls. 그녀는 인형을 많이 갖고 있다. → ______

10. The sun rise in the east. 태양은 동쪽에서 뜬다. → ______

11. I sleeps until 11 o'clock on weekends. → ______
난 주말에 11시까지 잔다.

12. They eats ice cream. 그들은 아이스크림을 먹는다. → ______

13. I likes warm hugs. → ______
난 따뜻한 포옹을 좋아해.

14. My mom always nag me. 엄마는 항상 내게 잔소리를 하신다. → ______

정답과 해설 p.3

Let's Practice More!

SET 07

학습목표 3 | 일반동사를 사용해 문장을 완성해 보아요.   공부한 날 :   맞은 개수 :   /20개

( ) 안의 동사를 이용해 문장을 완성해 보세요. (단, 필요하면 동사의 형태를 바꾸어 쓰세요.)

01. I ___hate___ shots. (hate)
난 주사가 싫어.

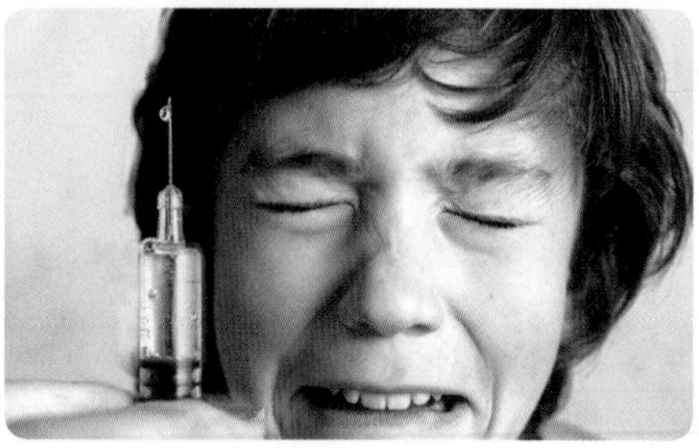

02. I __________ the flu. (have)
난 독감에 걸렸어.

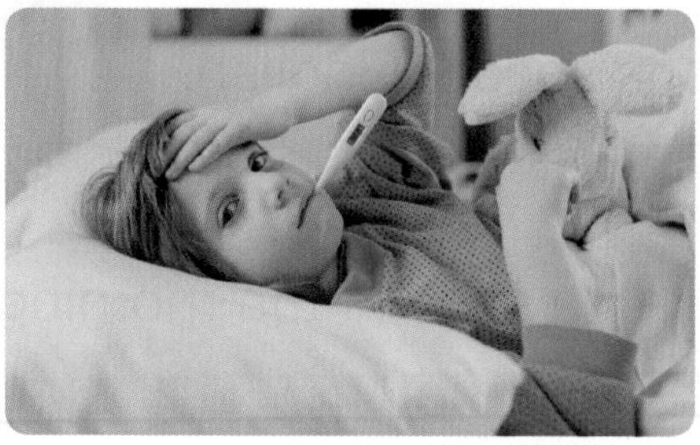

03. Mom __________ her up. (wake) 엄마가 그녀를 깨우셔.

04. They __________ cookies. (make) 그들은 쿠키를 만든다.

05. I __________ soccer with my friends. (play) 나는 친구들과 함께 축구를 해.

06. Mina __________ weekends. (like) 미나는 주말을 좋아한다.

07. She __________ up late at night. (stay) 그녀는 밤늦게까지 깨어있어.

08. They __________ hard these days. (study) 그들은 요즘 공부를 열심히 해.

09. I __________ a math test this Thursday. (have) 나는 이번 주 목요일에 수학시험을 쳐.

10. We __________ English. (teach) 우리는 영어를 가르친다.

정답과 해설 p.3

11. I __________ warm hugs. (like) 난 따뜻한 포옹을 좋아해.

12. We __________ many books. (read) 우리는 많은 책을 읽어.

13. He __________ "Detective Conan." (love) 그는 '명탐정 코난'을 아주 좋아해.

14. Many kids __________ cartoons on Sundays. (watch)
많은 아이들은 일요일에 만화를 본다.

15. You __________ very well. (swim) 너는 수영을 아주 잘 한다.

16. We __________ our homework first. (do) 우리는 숙제를 먼저 한다.

17. You __________ chocolate too much. (eat) 너는 초콜릿을 너무 많이 먹어.

18. I __________ up late. (get) 나는 늦게 일어난다.

19. He __________ baseball after school. (play)
그는 방과 후에 야구를 한다.

20. She __________ many dolls. (have)
그녀는 많은 인형을 갖고 있다.

정답과 해설 p.3

Let's Practice More!

SET 08

학습목표 3 | 일반동사를 사용해 문장을 완성해 보아요. 공부한 날 : 맞은 개수 : /20개

다음 주어진 문장의 주어를 ( )안의 주어로 바꿔 문장을 완성해 보세요. (단, 소유격 인칭대명사도 주어에 맞게 고쳐 쓰세요.)

01. I get up at seven. (He) 나는 7시에 일어나.

➔ He gets up at seven.

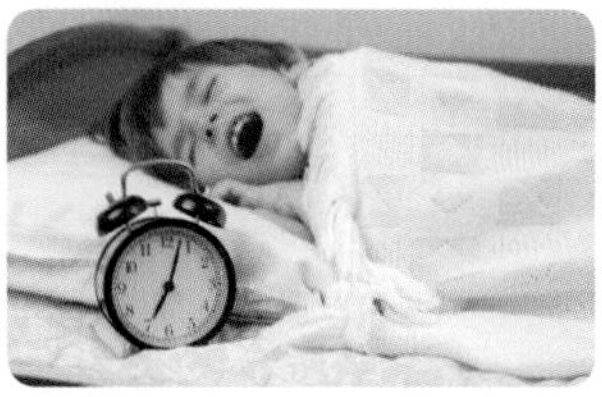

02. I put on my glasses. (She) 나는 나의 안경을 쓴다.

➔ ________________________________.

03. She listens to Exo's music. (I) 그녀는 엑소의 음악을 듣는다.

➔ ________________________________.

04. We want a vacation! (They) 우리는 방학을 원해!

➔ ________________________________!

05. I speak English very well. (He) 나는 영어를 아주 잘 해.

➔ ________________________________.

06. They have an English test next Monday. (He) 그들은 다음 주 월요일에 영어시험을 봐.

➔ ________________________________.

07. He does his homework after school. (I) 그는 방과 후에 그의 숙제를 한다.

➔ ________________________________.

08. I play computer games. (We) 나는 컴퓨터 게임을 한다.

➔ ________________________________.

09. We go to the movies every Saturday. (She) 우리는 토요일마다 영화를 보러 가.

➔ ________________________________.

10. I keep my smartphone at home. (Mina) 나는 집에서 스마트폰을 달고 산다.

➔ ________________________________.

정답과 해설 p.3

11. I eat breakfast with my family. (He) 나는 가족들과 아침을 먹는다.

➔ ______________________________.

12. I have a math test this Thursday. (They) 나는 이번 주 목요일에 수학시험을 쳐.

➔ ______________________________.

13. My children always nag me. (My mom)
내 아이들은 항상 내게 잔소리를 한다.

➔ ______________________________.

14. I need your help. (We) 나는 너의 도움이 필요해.

➔ ______________________________.

15. I dislike "Pororo." (Mom) 나는 '뽀로로'를 싫어해.

➔ ______________________________.

16. I go to school in a hurry. (You) 나는 서둘러 학교에 간다.

➔ ______________________________.

17. I like Sihu. (She) 나는 시후를 좋아해.

➔ ______________________________.

18. She has sweet dreams every night. (I) 그녀는 매일 밤 좋은 꿈을 꾼다.

➔ ______________________________.

19. I walk to school at eight. (We) 나는 8시에 걸어서 학교에 간다.

➔ ______________________________.

20. Mom, I have a fever. (She) 엄마, 내가 열나요.

➔ ______________________________.

정답과 해설 p.3

UNIT

일반동사의 3인칭 단수형 (1)

03 My mother works at the school.

❖ POiNT 1 ❖

주어가 3인칭 단수(He, She, It, Mina, Sihu)일 때, 일반동사의 모양을 바꿔 줘야 해요.

I study hard.
1인칭 주어
나는 열심히 공부해요.

You go to Seoul Elementary School.
2인칭 주어
당신은 서울 초등학교에 다녀요.

My mother works at the school.
3인칭 주어
우리 엄마는 학교에서 일해요.

❖ POiNT 2 ❖

대부분의 동사는 동사원형 끝에 -s를 붙이면 돼요! ⇨ 동사의 원래 형태+s

She wakes up early.
그녀는 일찍 일어나요.

She walks to work.
그녀는 걸어서 출근해요.

She says hello to the students.
그녀는 학생들에게 인사를 해요.

She prepares for the class. (*prepare for : ~을 준비하다)
그녀는 수업을 준비해요.

Check and Write

다음 주어진 동사를 알맞게 고쳐 빈칸에 써 보세요.

1. like

My mom likes watching TV.

나의 엄마는 TV를 보는 것을 좋아하셔.

2. want

Mina ______ a doll.

미나는 인형을 원해.

3. eat

My little brother ______ a lot.

내 남동생은 많이 먹어.

4. run

Nayeon ______ fast.

나연이는 빨리 달려.

5. drive

Dad ______ to his office.

아빠는 차를 타고 사무실로 가셔.

정답과 해설 p.3

UNIT

04 My sister studies hard.

일반동사의 3인칭 단수형 (2)

동사 뒤에 -s가 아니라 -es가 붙는 동사들도 있어요!

❖ POiNT 1 ❖

● **동사가 자음 + y로 끝나는 경우 : y를 i로 바꾸고 + -es를 붙여요!**

My sister studies hard.
나의 언니는 공부를 열심히 해요.

She tries her best.
그녀는 최선을 다해요.

❖ POiNT 2 ❖

● **동사가 -o, -s, -x, -ch, -sh로 끝나는 경우 : + -es를 붙여요!**

She always passes her exams.
그녀는 항상 시험을 통과해요.

She goes home after school.
그녀는 방과 후에 집으로 가요.

She finishes her homework first.
그녀는 먼저 그녀의 숙제를 끝내요.

She touches her pet.
그녀는 그녀의 애완동물을 만져요.

She relaxes on weekends.
그녀는 주말에 휴식을 취해요.

❖ POiNT 3 ❖

● **위의 규칙을 따르지 않는 동사가 있어요! have ⇨ 3인칭 주어 + has**

She has many dolls.
그녀는 많은 인형들을 가지고 있어요.

Check and Write

다음 주어진 동사를 알맞게 고쳐 빈칸에 써 보세요.

1. study

She studies hard.

그녀는 열심히 공부해.

2. go

Mina ______ to school by bus.

미나는 버스를 타고 학교로 가.

3. cry

Hayul ______ every morning.

하율이는 매일 아침 울어.

4. teach

She ______ English.

그녀는 영어를 가르치셔.

5. have

He ______ many books.

그는 많은 책을 가지고 있어.

정답과 해설 p.3

Practice 1 주어가 3인칭 단수일 때 일반동사의 형태를 익혀 보아요.

다음 문장에 알맞은 동사를 보기 에서 골라 알맞은 형태로 바꾸어 빈칸에 써 보세요. (중복 사용 가능)

A Dinner is ready!

보기			
clean	cut	put	wash
take out	say	make	open

1. My father __makes__ Bulgogi for dinner.
나의 아버지는 저녁으로 불고기를 만드셔.

2. He __________ the refrigerator. (*refrigerator : 냉장고)
그는 냉장고를 열어.

3. He __________ meat and vegetables. 그는 고기와 야채를 꺼내.

4. My mother __________ the vegetables. 나의 엄마는 야채를 씻어.

5. I __________ the onions. 나는 양파를 썰어.

6. Onions __________ me cry.
양파 때문에 나는 눈물이 나.

7. My brother __________ the table. 나의 오빠는 식탁을 청소해.

8. He __________ spoons and chopsticks on the table.
그는 식탁 위에 숟가락과 젓가락을 놓아.

9. My father __________, "Dinner is ready."
나의 아버지는 말씀하셔, "저녁식사가 준비됐단다."

정답과 해설 p.3

B Mina's weekend

보기			
go	work	watch	love
study	teach	like	play

1. My mom __________ at the school. 나의 엄마는 학교에서 일하셔.

2. She __________ students science. 그녀는 학생들에게 과학을 가르치셔.

3. My brother __________ to college. 나의 오빠는 대학에 다녀.

4. He __________ computer science. 그는 컴퓨터 과학을 공부해.

5. My sister __________ the violin. 나의 언니는 바이올린을 연주해.

6. She __________ taking pictures. 그녀는 사진 찍는 걸 아주 좋아해.

7. My grandma __________ TV all day.
나의 할머니는 하루 종일 TV를 보셔.

8. She __________ Korean dramas.
그녀는 한국 드라마를 좋아하셔.

C How do they get to work?

보기 take drive walk ride

1. My father __________ his car. 나의 아빠는 차를 운전하셔.

2. My brother __________ his bicycle.
나의 오빠는 자전거를 타.

3. My mother __________ a taxi. 나의 엄마는 택시를 타셔.

4. My sister __________ to school. 나의 언니는 걸어서 통학해.

정답과 해설 p.3

Practice 2 알맞은 형태의 일반동사를 써서 문장을 완성해 보아요.

다음 우리말 뜻과 같도록 주어진 표현을 순서에 맞게 배열하여 문장을 완성하세요.

1. (has, an answer, Every puzzle).

모든 퍼즐은 해답을 가지고 있어.

→ Every puzzle has an answer.

2. (kisses, me, My dog).

나의 개는 나에게 뽀뽀를 해.

→ ______________________.

3. (solves, the problem, He). 그는 문제를 해결해.

→ ______________________.

4. (Nintendo, Junsu, wants). 준수는 닌텐도를 원해요.

→ ______________________.

5. (board games, Sihu, plays). 시후는 보드게임을 한다.

→ ______________________.

6. (likes playing, board games, He). 그는 보드게임 하는 것을 좋아한다.

→ ______________________.

7. (math, My teacher, teaches). 나의 선생님은 수학을 가르치셔.

→ ______________________.

8. (does, his homework, Sihu) after school. 시후는 방과 후에 그의 숙제를 해.

→ ______________________ after school.

정답과 해설 p.3

9. (Nayeon, board games, plays). 나연이는 보드게임을 해.

➔ ____.

10. (board games, play, I) with Nayeon. 나는 나연이랑 보드게임을 해.

➔ ___________________________ with Nayeon.

11. (me, scolds, Mom). (*scold : 혼내다, 꾸짖다) 엄마는 나를 혼내셔.

➔ __________________________________.

12. Whenever I get too happy, (always happens, something bad).

내가 엄청 행복할 때마다 나쁜 일이 항상 생기거든. (*whenever : ~할 때마다)

➔ Whenever I get too happy, ___________________________.

13. *Little Red Riding Hood*: Grandmother! (Your voice, so odd, sounds).

빨간 망토 소녀 : 할머니! 목소리가 너무 이상하게 들려요. (*odd : 이상한)

The wolf: Oh, I just have a cold.

늑대 : 오, 난 그저 감기에 걸린 거란다.

➔ *Little Red Riding Hood*: Grandmother! ______________________.

14. (saves, nine, A stitch in time).

제때의 바느질 한 번이 아홉 번의 바느질을 던다.

➔ __________________________________.

15. (The early bird, the worm, catches). (*worm : 벌레)

일찍 일어나는 새가 벌레를 잡는다.

➔ ____.

16. (has, so many lessons, The world). 세상은 아주 많은 교훈을 가지고 있다.

➔ ____.

정답과 해설 p.3

Practice 3 주어에 알맞게 일반동사를 바꾸어 완전한 문장을 써 보아요.

우리말 뜻을 참고하여 주어진 표현을 사용해 문장을 영어로 완성해 보세요.
(주어가 3인칭 단수일 때는 동사를 바꿔 쓰세요.)

1. (A firefighter, save, many lives)
소방관은 많은 생명을 살려요.

→ A firefighter saves many lives.

2. (A mailman, deliver, letters)
우체부는 편지를 배달해요.

→ ______________________________.

3. (My mother, wash, the vegetables) 나의 엄마는 야채를 씻어요.
→ ______________________________.

4. (cut, the onions) 나는 양파를 썰어요.
→ ______________________________.

5. (Every puzzle, have, an answer) 모든 퍼즐은 해답을 가지고 있어요.
→ ______________________________.

6. (A firefighter, wear, an orange uniform) 소방관은 주황색 유니폼을 입어요.
→ ______________________________.

7. (Mina, send, a letter) 미나는 편지를 보내요.
→ ______________________________.

8. (Sihu, write a letter, to Mina) 시후는 미나에게 편지를 써요.
→ ______________________________.

9. (My homeroom teacher, teach, English) 나의 담임 선생님은 영어를 가르치세요.
→ ______________________________.

정답과 해설 p.3

10. (A panda, eat, bamboo leaves)
판다가 대나무 잎을 먹어요.

➔ ______________________________.

11. (My grandpa, read, books)
나의 할아버지는 책을 읽어요.

➔ ______________________________.

12. (Mina, dislike, going to the dentist) 미나는 치과에 가는 것을 싫어해요.

➔ ____.

13. (brush, her teeth, three times a day)
그녀는 하루에 세 번 양치를 해요.

➔ ____.

14. (say hello to, the students) 그녀는 학생들에게 인사를 해요.

➔ ____.

15. (have, a good voice) 그는 좋은 목소리를 가지고 있어요.

➔ ____.

16. (Mina, drink, milk, for breakfast) 미나는 아침으로 우유를 마셔요.

➔ ____.

17. (Bakers, bake, bread) 제빵사들은 빵을 구워요.

➔ ____.

18. (Mina, love, bread) 미나는 빵을 아주 좋아해요.

➔ ____.

19. (My younger brother, copy, pandas) 내 남동생은 판다를 따라 해요.

➔ ____.

정답과 해설 p.4

Let's Practice More!

SET 01

학습목표 1 | **일반동사의 3인칭 단수형의 다양한 형태를 연습해 보아요.** 공부한 날 : 맞은 개수 : /12개

다음 밑줄 친 부분이 맞으면 ○표, 틀리면 ×표를 하세요.

01. My brother studys math. 우리 오빠는 수학을 공부해. → ×

02. My father makes Bulgogi for dinner. → ______
나의 아버지는 저녁으로 불고기를 만드신다.

03. He openes the refrigerator. → ______
그는 냉장고를 연다.

04. He takes out meat and vegetables. 그는 고기와 야채를 꺼낸다. → ______

05. My mother washs the vegetables. → ______
엄마는 야채를 씻으신다.

06. My brother cleans the table. → ______
내 남동생은 탁자를 청소한다.

07. My mom works at the school. 나의 엄마는 학교에서 일하신다. → ______

08. He puts spoons and chopsticks on the table. → ______
그는 식탁 위에 숟가락과 젓가락을 놓는다.

09. My father sayes, "Dinner is ready." → ______
나의 아버지는 말씀하신다, "저녁식사가 준비됐단다."

10. She teachs science. 그녀는 과학을 가르친다. → ______

11. My brother goes to college. → ______
나의 오빠는 대학에 다닌다.

12. Sihu playes board games. → ______
시후는 보드게임을 한다.

정답과 해설 p.4

Let's Practice More!

SET 02

학습목표 1 | 일반동사의 3인칭 단수형의 다양한 형태를 연습해 보아요. 공부한 날 : 맞은 개수 : /12개

( ) 안에서 알맞은 것을 골라 보세요.

01. She (touches / touchs) a baby. 그녀는 아기를 만진다.

02. He (studys / studies) science. 그는 과학을 공부한다.

03. Your voice (sounds / soundes) so odd.
너의 목소리가 너무 이상하게 들린다.

04. The early bird (catchs / catches) the worm. 일찍 일어나는 새가 벌레를 잡는다.

05. She (brushs / brushes) her teeth three times a day.
그녀는 하루에 세 번 양치를 한다.

06. My younger brother (copys / copies) pandas. 내 남동생은 판다를 따라 한다.

07. A mailman (delivers / deliveres) letters. 우체부는 편지를 배달한다.

08. My grandma (watchs / watches) TV all day.
나의 할머니는 하루 종일 TV를 보신다.

09. The baker (bake / bakes) bread. 그 제빵사는 빵을 굽는다.

10. Something bad always (happenes / happens). 나쁜 일은 항상 일어난다.

11. She (tryes / tries) her best. 그녀는 최선을 다한다.

12. My dad (relaxs / relaxes) on weekends.
나의 아빠는 주말에 휴식을 취한다.

정답과 해설 p.4

Let's Practice More!

SET 03

학습목표 1 | 일반동사의 3인칭 단수형의 다양한 형태를 연습해 보아요.   공부한 날 :   맞은 개수 :   /14개

다음 밑줄 친 부분을 올바르게 고쳐 보세요.

01. She <u>haves</u> a pretty doll. → has
그녀는 예쁜 인형이 있다.

02. He <u>dos</u> his homework. → ________
그는 그의 숙제를 한다.

03. He <u>studys</u> science. 그는 과학을 공부한다. → ________

04. My sister <u>playes</u> the violin. → ________
나의 언니는 바이올린을 연주한다.

05. Mike <u>trys</u> his best. → ________
Mike는 최선을 다한다.

06. My grandma <u>watchs</u> TV all day. 나의 할머니는 하루 종일 TV를 보신다. → ________

07. Your voice <u>soundes</u> so odd. 너의 목소리가 너무 이상하게 들린다. → ________

08. He <u>walkes</u> to school. 그는 걸어서 학교에 간다. → ________

09. My homeroom teacher <u>teachs</u> English. → ________
나의 담임 선생님은 영어를 가르치신다.

10. She <u>saies</u> hello to the students. 그녀는 학생들에게 인사를 한다. → ________

11. She <u>brushs</u> her teeth three times a day. → ________
그녀는 하루에 세 번 양치를 한다.

12. Mina <u>drinkes</u> milk for breakfast. → ________
미나는 아침으로 우유를 마신다.

13. Jane <u>wantes</u> a doll. Jane은 인형을 원한다. → ________

14. My mom <u>helpes</u> me. 나의 엄마는 나를 도와주신다. → ________

정답과 해설 p.4

Let's Practice More!

SET 04

학습목표 2 | 주어에 따라 달라지는 일반 동사의 현재형을 연습해 보아요. 공부한 날 : 맞은 개수 : /12개

다음 밑줄 친 부분이 맞으면 ○표, 틀리면 ×표를 하세요.

01. Junsu wants Nintendo. 준수는 닌텐도를 원한다. → ○

02. Sihu and Junwoo does their homework after school. →
시후와 준우는 방과 후에 그들의 숙제를 한다.

03. I play board games with Nayeon. 나는 나연이랑 보드게임을 한다. →

04. Mom scold me. →
엄마는 나를 혼내신다.

05. The world have many lessons. 세상은 많은 교훈들을 가지고 있다. →

06. A stitch in time saves nine. 제때의 바느질 한 번이 아홉 번의 바느질을 던다. →

07. Her friends likes Korean dramas. →
그녀의 친구들은 한국 드라마를 좋아한다.

08. My father drives his car. 나의 아빠는 차를 운전하신다. →

09. My brother ride his bicycle. →
나의 오빠는 자전거를 탄다.

10. My mother takes a taxi. 나의 엄마는 택시를 타신다. →

11. My younger sister copy lions. 나의 여동생은 사자를 따라 한다. →

12. My dog kisses me. →
나의 개는 나에게 뽀뽀를 한다.

정답과 해설 p.4

Let's Practice More!

SET 05

학습목표 2 | 주어에 따라 달라지는 일반 동사의 현재형을 연습해 보아요. 공부한 날 : 맞은 개수 : /14개

( ) 안에서 알맞은 것을 골라 보세요.

01. We (like / likes) weekends. 우리는 주말을 좋아한다.

02. A firefighter (save / saves) many lives.
소방관은 많은 생명을 살린다.

03. The class (begin / begins) at 9 o'clock. 수업은 9시에 시작한다.

04. They (wake / wakes) up early. 그들은 일찍 일어난다.

05. Firefighters (wear / wears) orange uniforms. 소방관들은 주황색 유니폼을 입는다.

06. Mina (send / sends) a letter. 미나는 편지를 보낸다.

07. A panda (eat / eats) bamboo leaves.
판다는 대나무 잎을 먹는다.

08. My grandpa (read / reads) books. 나의 할아버지는 책을 읽으신다.

09. Mina (dislike / dislikes) going to the dentist.
미나는 치과에 가는 것을 싫어한다.

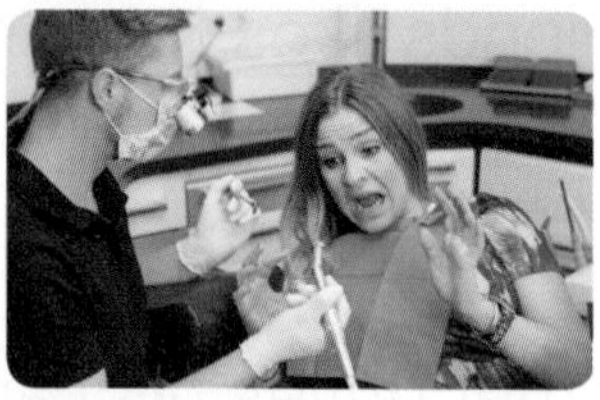

10. We (brush / brushes) our teeth three times a day.
우리는 하루에 세 번 양치를 한다.

11. My homeroom teacher (teach / teaches) English.
나의 담임 선생님은 영어를 가르치신다.

12. Students (say / says) hello to her. 학생들은 그녀에게 인사를 한다.

13. He (have / has) a good voice. 그는 좋은 목소리를 가지고 있다.

14. They (play / plays) board games with Nayeon.
그들은 나연이와 보드게임을 한다.

정답과 해설 p.4

Let's Practice More!

SET 06

CH 01

학습목표 2 | 주어에 따라 달라지는 일반 동사의 현재형을 연습해 보아요. 공부한 날 : 맞은 개수 : /14개

다음 문장을 읽고 밑줄 친 부분을 올바르게 고쳐 보세요.

01. The math teacher give us homework. → gives
그 수학 선생님은 우리에게 숙제를 내주신다.

02. Nayeon play with dolls. → ________
나연이는 인형놀이를 한다.

03. He solve the problem. 그는 문제를 해결한다. → ________

04. My mom work at the school. → ________
나의 엄마는 학교에서 일하신다.

05. She teach science. 그녀는 과학을 가르친다. → ________

06. My brother go to college. 나의 오빠는 대학에 다닌다. → ________

07. He study Japanese. 그는 일본어를 공부한다. → ________

08. My sister play the violin. 나의 언니는 바이올린을 연주한다. → ________

09. He love taking pictures. → ________
그는 사진 찍는 걸 아주 좋아한다.

10. My grandma watch TV all day. 나의 할머니는 하루 종일 TV를 보신다. → ________

11. She like Korean dramas. 그녀는 한국 드라마를 좋아한다. → ________

12. My father drive his car. → ________
나의 아빠는 차를 운전하신다.

13. My brother ride his bicycle. 나의 오빠는 자전거를 탄다. → ________

14. My mother take a taxi. 나의 엄마는 택시를 타신다. → ________

정답과 해설 p.4

Let's Practice More!

SET 07

학습목표 3 | **일반 동사를 사용해 문장을 완성해 보아요.** 공부한 날 : 맞은 개수 : /20개

( ) 안의 동사원형을 이용해 문장을 완성해 보세요.

01. She touches her cat. (touch)
그녀는 그녀의 고양이를 만진다.

02. A mailman ________ letters. (deliver)
우체부는 편지를 배달한다.

03. My father ________ Bulgogi for dinner. (make)
나의 아버지는 저녁으로 불고기를 만드신다.

04. He ________ the refrigerator. (open) 그는 냉장고를 연다.

05. He ________ out meat and vegetables. (take) 그는 고기와 야채를 꺼낸다.

06. My mother ________ the vegetables. (wash) 나의 엄마는 야채를 씻으신다.

07. She ________ the onions. (cut) 그녀는 양파를 썬다.

08. My brother ________ the table. (clean)
나의 오빠는 식탁을 청소한다.

09. He ________ spoons and chopsticks on the table. (put)
그는 식탁 위에 숟가락과 젓가락을 놓는다.

정답과 해설 p.4

10. My father ___________, "Dinner is ready." (say)
나의 아버지는 말씀하신다, "저녁식사가 준비됐단다."

11. Mom ___________ me. (scold) 엄마는 나를 혼내신다.

12. The world ___________ many lessons. (have) 세상은 많은 교훈을 가지고 있다.

13. Your voice ___________ so odd. (sound) 너의 목소리가 너무 이상하게 들린다.

14. A stitch in time ___________ nine. (save) 제때의 바느질 한 번이 아홉 번의 바느질을 던다.

15. The early bird ___________ the worm. (catch) 일찍 일어나는 새가 벌레를 잡는다.

16. He ___________ soccer with Nayeon. (play) 그는 나연이와 축구를 한다.

17. A firefighter ___________ many lives. (save) 소방관은 많은 생명을 살린다.

18. The class ___________ at 9 o'clock. (begin) 수업은 9시에 시작한다.

19. He ___________ up early. (wake)
그는 일찍 일어난다.

20. Something bad always ___________. (happen)
나쁜 일은 항상 일어난다.

정답과 해설 p.4

Let's Practice More!

SET 08

학습목표 3 | **일반 동사를 사용해 문장을 완성해 보아요.** 공부한 날 : 맞은 개수 : /20개

다음 주어진 문장의 주어를 ( )안의 주어로 바꿔 전체 문장을 완성해 보세요.

01. I play in the playground. (He)
나는 운동장에서 논다.

→ He plays in the playground.

02. They read books. (My grandfather)
그들은 책을 읽는다.

→ ______________________.

03. We drink milk for breakfast. (Mina) 우리는 아침으로 우유를 마신다.

→ ______________________.

04. Bakers bake bread. (He) 제빵사들은 빵을 굽는다.

→ ______________________.

05. I love bread. (She) 나는 빵을 아주 좋아한다.

→ ______________________.

06. They copy pandas. (My younger brother) 그들은 판다를 따라 한다.

→ ______________________.

07. I prepare for the class. (She) 나는 수업을 준비한다.

→ ______________________.

08. My parents relax on weekends. (My dad) 나의 부모님은 주말에 휴식을 취하신다.

→ ______________________.

정답과 해설 p.4

09. Mina's friends write a letter to her. (Sihu) 미나의 친구들은 그녀에게 편지를 쓴다.

➔ ____.

10. They help me. (My mom) 그들은 나를 도와준다.

➔ ____.

11. Many people try their best. (She) 많은 사람들은 최선을 다한다.

➔ ____.

12. We want a doll. (Jane) 우리는 인형을 원한다.

➔ ____.

13. They watch TV all day. (My grandma) 그들은 하루 종일 TV를 본다.

➔ ____.

14. My classmates send a letter. (Mina) 나의 반 친구들은 편지를 보낸다.

➔ ____.

15. Animals eat bamboo leaves. (A panda) 동물들은 대나무 잎을 먹는다.

➔ ____.

16. Some children dislike going to the dentist. (He) 몇몇의 아이들은 치과에 가는 것을 싫어한다.

➔ ____.

17. I teach English. (My homeroom teacher) 나는 영어를 가르친다.

➔ ____.

18. Books have many lessons. (The world) 책들은 많은 교훈을 가지고 있다.

➔ ____.

19. All members have a good voice. (My brother) 모든 구성원들이 좋은 목소리를 가지고 있다.

➔ ____.

20. I scold him. (She) 나는 그를 혼낸다.

➔ ____.

정답과 해설 p.4

Chapter 02 be동사의 부정문과 의문문

이 챕터에서는 be동사의 부정문과 축약형,
그리고 be동사의 의문문과 그에 대한 대답에 대해 배워 보아요.

☆ 학습 방향 및 배울 내용 미리보기 ☆

☐ **Unit 01 : We are not late.**

be동사의 부정문

be동사의 부정문을 만드는 방법과 줄여 쓰는 방법에 대해 알아보아요.

▼

☐ **Unit 02 : Are you hungry?**

be동사의 의문문

be동사의 의문문을 만드는 방법과 be동사 의문문에 대답하는 방법에 대해 배워 보아요.

단어 미리보기

이 챕터에 나올 단어들 중 이미 알고 있는 단어가 있나요?
맞는 뜻을 골라 체크해 봐요.

날짜 : 이름 : 알고 있는 단어의 수 : /24개

No.	아는 단어	단어	품사	알맞은 뜻에 체크 표시해 봐요.			
1	☑	city	명사	도시	☑	마을	☐
2	☐	happy	형용사	슬픈	☐	행복한	☐
3	☐	house	명사	말	☐	집	☐
4	☐	young	형용사	어린	☐	나이 많은	☐
5	☐	bird	명사	새	☐	오리	☐
6	☐	easy	형용사	어려운	☐	쉬운	☐
7	☐	same	형용사	같은	☐	다른	☐
8	☐	funny	형용사	화난	☐	웃긴	☐
9	☐	baby	명사	사람	☐	아기	☐
10	☐	hungry	형용사	배고픈	☐	배부른	☐
11	☐	angry	형용사	웃긴	☐	화난	☐
12	☐	friend	명사	친구	☐	어른	☐
13	☐	cat	명사	강아지	☐	고양이	☐
14	☐	dancer	명사	가수	☐	무용수	☐
15	☐	sister	명사	오빠	☐	여자형제	☐
16	☐	soccer	명사	축구	☐	농구	☐
17	☐	little	형용사	(크기가) 작은	☐	(크기가) 큰	☐
18	☐	teacher	명사	학생	☐	선생	☐
19	☐	parents	명사	부모	☐	자식	☐
20	☐	child	명사	아이	☐	어른	☐
21	☐	clean	형용사	더러운	☐	깨끗한	☐
22	☐	important	형용사	사소한	☐	중요한	☐
23	☐	smart	형용사	똑똑한	☐	서투른	☐
24	☐	fast	형용사	빠른	☐	느린	☐

UNIT

01 We are not late.

be동사의 부정문

❖ POiNT ❖

be동사의 부정문은 be동사 다음에 not을 써요.

be동사 + not은 줄여 쓸 수 있어요! 단, am not은 줄여 쓰지 않아요!

I	am not	⇨	I'm not
he	is not		he isn't
she			she isn't
it			it isn't
we	are not		we aren't
you			you aren't
they			they aren't

I am a grown-up. 나는 어른이야.

I am not a grown-up. 나는 어른이 아니야.

He is in the Internet cafe. 그는 PC방에 있어.

He is not in the Internet cafe. 그는 PC방에 있지 않아.

= He isn't in the Internet cafe.

We are late. 우리는 늦었어.

We are not late. 우리는 늦지 않았어.

= We aren't late.

Check and Write

다음 빈칸에 알맞은 be동사의 부정형을 채워보세요.

1. She **is not** a grown-up.
   She **isn't** a grown-up.
   그녀는 어른이 아니야.

2. I _____ a fool!
   난 바보가 아니야!

3. They _____ in the classroom.
   They _____ in the classroom.
   그들은 교실에 있지 않아.

4. He _____ sleepy.
   He _____ sleepy. 그는 졸리지 않아.

5. We _____ bored.
   We _____ bored. 우리들은 지루하지 않아.

6. The baby _____ awake.
   The baby _____ awake.
   그 아기는 깨어있지 않아.

정답과 해설 p.5

UNIT 02 Are you hungry?

be동사의 의문문

❖ POiNT ❖

be동사의 의문문은 주어와 be동사의 순서를 바꾸고 끝에 물음표를 써요.
대답은 맞으면 "Yes, 주어+be동사.", 틀리면 "No, 주어+be동사+not(의 줄임)."으로 해요.

You are hungry.
너는 ~이다 배고픈

Are you hungry?
~이니 너는 배고픈

Yes, I am.
응, 나는 배고파.

No, I'm not.
아니, 나는 배고프지 않아.

They are in the classroom.
그들은 있다 교실에

Are they in the classroom?
있니 그들은 교실에

Yes, they are.
응, 그들은 교실에 있어.

No, they aren't.
아니, 그들은 교실에 있지 않아.

She is angry.
그녀는 ~이다 화난

Is she angry?
~이니 그녀는 화난

Yes, she is.
응, 그녀는 화났어.

No, she isn't.
아니, 그녀는 화나지 않았어.

Check and Write

다음 문장을 의문문으로 바꾸고 그에 대한 대답을 완성해 보세요.

1. She is your friend. 그녀는 네 친구다.

⇨ [Is] she your friend? 그녀는 네 친구니?

- Yes, she [is].
- No, she [isn't].

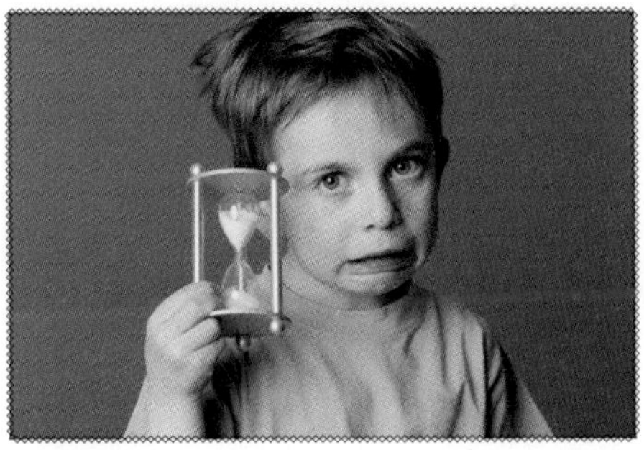

2. You are late. 너는 늦었다.

⇨ [ ] you late? 너 늦었니?

- Yes, I [ ].
- No, [ ] [ ].

3. He is at home. 그는 집에 있다.

⇨ [ ] he at home? 그는 집에 있어?

- Yes, he [ ].
- No, he [ ].

4. It is a cat. 그것은 고양이다.

⇨ [ ] it a cat? 그것은 고양이야?

- Yes, it [ ].
- No, it [ ].

정답과 해설 p.5

Practice 1 be동사의 부정문과 의문문을 익혀 보아요.

우리말 뜻을 참고하여 빈칸에 be동사를 알맞게 바꿔 문장을 완성해 보세요.

A Who is Irene?

1. Irene ___is___ ___not___ a grown-up.
   Irene은 어른이 아니다.

2. She ________ ________ a picky eater. (*picky eater: 입맛이 까다로운 사람)
   그녀는 입맛이 까다로운 사람이 아니다.

3. ________ she a good dancer?
   그녀는 춤을 잘 추니?

4. No, she ________ ________.
   아니, 그녀는 잘 추지 않아.

5. She ________ ________ a good dancer, but she is a good singer.
   그녀는 춤은 잘 못 추지만 노래를 잘 부른다.

6. ________ her sister kind?
   그녀의 여동생은 친절해?

7. Yes, she ________.
   응, 그녀는 친절해.

8. ________ her brothers students?
   그녀의 오빠들은 학생이니?

9. No, they ________ ________ students.
   아니, 그들은 학생이 아니야.

정답과 해설 p.5

B Who is Minho?

1. Minho __________ __________ funny.
   민호는 재밌지 않아.

2. __________ he a soccer player?
   그는 축구선수야?

3. Yes, but he __________ __________ fast.
   그래, 그렇지만 그는 빠르지 않아.

4. __________ his little sister in Seoul?
   그의 여동생은 서울에 있어?

5. Yes, she __________ in Seoul.
   그래, 그녀는 서울에 있어.

6. His sister __________ __________ tall.
   그의 여동생은 키가 크지 않아.

7. She __________ __________ mean.
   그녀는 심술궂지 않아. (*mean: 심술궂은, 짓궂은)

C Who is Ken?

1. __________ Ken lazy?
   Ken은 게으르니?

2. No, he __________ __________ lazy.
   아니, 그는 게으르지 않아.

3. __________ his teacher strict? (*strict: 엄격한)
   그의 선생님은 엄격해?

4. No, she __________ __________ strict.
   아니, 그녀는 엄격하지 않아.

정답과 해설 p.5

Practice 2 표현을 알맞게 배열해서 be동사의 부정문과 의문문을 완성해 보아요.

다음 우리말 뜻과 같도록 주어진 표현을 순서에 맞게 배열하여 문장을 완성하세요.

1. (your parents, Are, over there)? 너의 부모님은 저기 계시니?
   ➔ Are your parents over there?

2. (your parents, strict, Are)? (*strict: 엄격한)
   너의 부모님은 엄격하시니?
   ➔ ______________________________?

3. (your father, Is, a good singer)? 너의 아버지는 노래를 잘 부르시니?
   ➔ ______________________________?

4. (grandparents' house, Is, your) in the city?
   너의 조부모님 댁은 도시에 있니?
   ➔ ______________________________ in the city?

5. (My brother, smart, not, is). 우리 형은 똑똑하지 않아.
   ➔ ______________________________.

6. (Hayul, a picky eater, Is)? 하율이는 편식하니? (입맛이 까다롭니?)
   ➔ ______________________________?

7. (is, Hayul, a grown-up, not). 하율이는 어른이 아니야.
   ➔ ______________________________.

8. (I, not, happy, am). 나는 행복하지 않다.
   ➔ ______________________________.

9. (not, is, He, a child) anymore. 그는 더 이상 어린아이가 아니야.
   ➔ ______________________________ anymore.

정답과 해설 p.5

10. (you, Are, tired)? 너는 피곤하니?

➔ ______________________________?

11. (am, a big eater, I, not). 나는 대식가가 아니야.

➔ ______________________________.

12. (not, inside the house, My mother, is). 우리 엄마는 집 안에 안 계세요.

➔ ______________________________.

13. (not, far away, Happiness, is). 행복은 멀리 있지 않아.

➔ ______________________________.

14. (not, They, are, young). 그들은 어리지 않아.

➔ ______________________________.

15. (your real friends, not, They, are). 그들은 너의 진정한 친구들이 아니야.

➔ ______________________________.

16. (your, not, enemy, I'm).
나는 너의 적이 아니다.

➔ ______________________________
______________________________.

17. (not, You, weak, are).
너는 약하지 않아.

➔ ______________________________
______________________________.

18. (sad, Are, you)? 너 슬프니?

➔ ______________________________?

19. (you, Are, sure)? 확실해요?

➔ ______________________________?

Practice 3 be동사가 쓰인 부정문과 의문문을 써 보아요.

우리말 뜻을 참고하여 주어진 표현을 사용해 문장을 영어로 완성해 보세요.

1. (be afraid of, birds)
당신은 새를 무서워하나요?

→ Are you afraid of birds
______________________?

2. (lazy)
난 게으르지 않아.

→ ______________________
______________________.

3. (easy) 그것은 쉽지 않아.
→ ______________________.

4. (thirsty) 너 목마르니?
→ ______________________?

5. (be late for) 너는 학교에 늦니?
→ ______________________?

6. (hungry) 너희들은 배가 고프니?
→ ______________________?

7. (hungry) 아니, 우리는 배고프지 않아.
→ ______________________.

8. (Sehun, a good rapper) 세훈이는 랩을 잘하지 못한다.
→ ______________________.

정답과 해설 p.5

9. (a good rapper) 너는 랩을 잘하니?

➔ ____?

10. (a good rapper) 나는 랩을 못해.

➔ ____.

11. (best friend) 그는 너의 가장 친한 친구니?

➔ ____?

12. (best friend) 아니, 그는 내 가장 친한 친구가 아니야.

➔ ____.

13. (in the same class) 우리는 같은 반이 아니다.

➔ ____.

14. (classroom, clean) 우리 교실은 깨끗하지 않다.

➔ ____.

15. (the problem, important) 그 문제가 중요하니?

➔ ____?

16. (the webtoon, funny) 그 웹툰 재미있니?

➔ ____?

17. (The webtoon, funny) 그 웹툰은 재미없어.

➔ ____.

정답과 해설 p.5

Let's Practice More!

SET 01

학습목표 1 | **be동사의 부정문 형태를 연습해 보아요.** 공부한 날 : 맞은 개수 : /12개

다음 문장을 읽고 밑줄 친 부분이 맞으면 ○표, 틀리면 ×표 하세요.

01. I <u>am not</u> happy.
나는 행복하지 않아.

→ ○

02. I <u>not am</u> a kid anymore.
나는 더 이상 어린애가 아니야.

→ ______

03. She <u>not is</u> a teacher. 그녀는 선생님이 아니야. → ______

04. He <u>are not</u> rich. 그는 부유하지 않아. → ______

05. They <u>are not</u> young. 그들은 어리지 않아. → ______

06. You <u>are not</u> a grown-up. 너는 어른이 아니야. → ______

07. It <u>am not</u> long. 그것은 길지 않아. → ______

08. She <u>is not</u> inside the house. 그녀는 집 안에 있지 않아. → ______

09. He <u>not is</u> mean. 그는 심술궂지 않아. → ______

10. We <u>are not</u> angry. 우리는 화나지 않았어. → ______

11. They <u>are not</u> kind. 그들은 친절하지 않아. → ______

12. You <u>not are</u> a fool. 너는 바보가 아니야. → ______

정답과 해설 p.5

Let's Practice More!

SET 02

학습목표 1 | be동사의 부정문 형태를 연습해 보아요.　　공부한 날 :　　맞은 개수 :　　/14개

다음 ( ) 안에서 알맞은 것을 골라 보세요.

01. I (am not / is not) a picky eater. 난 입맛이 까다로운 사람이 아니야.

02. Happiness (am not / is not) far away. 행복은 멀리 있지 않아.

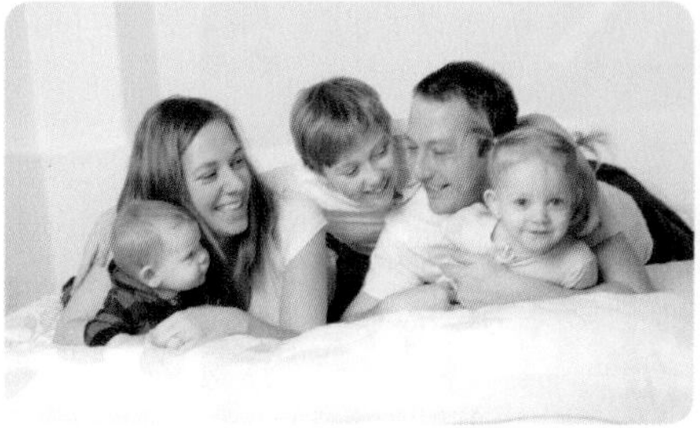

03. She (is not / not is) kind. 그녀는 친절하지 않아.

04. He (am not / is not) fast. 그는 빠르지 않아.

05. They (not are / are not) your real friends. 그들은 너의 진정한 친구들이 아니야.

06. I (am not / is not) lazy. 나는 게으르지 않아.

07. It (not is / is not) easy. 그것은 쉽지 않아.

08. We (is not / are not) twins. 우리는 쌍둥이가 아니야.

09. The baby (is not / not is) awake. 그 아기는 깨어있지 않아.

10. It (is not / are not) fresh. 그것은 신선하지 않아.

11. You (not are / are not) weak. 너는 약하지 않아.

12. Sihu (is not / not is) a good rapper. 시후는 좋은 래퍼가 아니야.

13. We (is not / are not) in the same class. 우리는 같은 반이 아니야.

14. Our classroom (is not / not is) clean. 우리 교실은 깨끗하지 않아.

정답과 해설 p.5

Let's Practice More!

SET 03

학습목표 2 | be동사의 부정문은 줄여 쓸 수 있어요. 공부한 날 : 맞은 개수 : /14개

밑줄 친 부분을 줄여서 써 보세요.

01. My older brother is not smart.
나의 형은 똑똑하지 않아.

→ isn't

02. I am not your enemy.
나는 너의 적이 아니야.

→ ______

03. Irene is not a grown-up. Irene은 어른이 아니야. → ______

04. She is not a picky eater. 그녀는 입맛이 까다로운 사람이 아니야. → ______

05. He is not a good dancer. 그는 좋은 댄서가 아니야. → ______

06. They are not students. 그들은 학생들이 아니야. → ______

07. He is not funny. 그는 웃기지 않아. → ______

08. She is not in Seoul. 그녀는 서울에 있지 않아. → ______

09. We are not rich. 우리는 부유하지 않아. → ______

10. We are not hungry. 우리는 배고프지 않아. → ______

11. He is not my best friend. 그는 나의 가장 친한 친구가 아니야. → ______

12. I am not sleepy. 나는 졸리지 않아. → ______

13. They are not in Korea. 그들은 한국에 있지 않아. → ______

14. You are not happy. 너는 행복하지 않아. → ______

정답과 해설 p.5

Let's Practice More!

SET 04

학습목표 3 | be동사의 의문문을 연습해 보아요. 공부한 날 : 맞은 개수 : /12개

다음 빈칸에 am, are, is 중 알맞은 것을 채워보세요.

01. ___Are___ you tired? 너 피곤하니?

02. ________ your father a good singer? 너희 아버지는 노래를 잘 하시니?

03. ________ he funny? 그는 웃기니?

04. ________ her sister kind? 그녀의 여동생은 친절하니?

05. ________ her brothers students? 그녀의 남자 형제들은 학생이니?

06. ________ he a soccer player? 그는 축구선수니?

07. ________ I old? 내가 나이가 들었니?

08. ________ your parents over there? 너희 부모님은 저쪽에 계시니?

09. ________ she strict? 그녀는 엄격하니?

10. ________ you sure? 너 확신하니?

11. ________ we late for school? 우리 학교에 늦었니?

12. ________ she afraid of birds? 그녀는 새를 무서워하니?

정답과 해설 p.6

Let's Practice More!

SET 05

학습목표 3 | **be동사의 의문문을 연습해 보아요.** 공부한 날 : 맞은 개수 : /14개

주어진 문장을 의문문으로 바꿔 보세요.

01. You are thirsty.

➔ Are you thirsty ?

너는 목마르니?

02. She is angry.

➔ ____________________?

그녀는 화났니?

03. She is a good singer.

➔ ____________________?

그녀는 노래를 잘 부르니?

04. Their house is in the city.

➔ ____________________?

그들의 집은 도시에 있니?

05. The webtoon is funny.

➔ ____________________?

그 웹툰은 재미있니?

06. You are hungry.

➔ ____________________?

너는 배고프니?

07. They are your friends.

➔ ____________________?

그들은 너의 친구들이니?

정답과 해설 p.6

08. He is a teacher.

➔ ____?

그는 선생님이니?

09. The problem is important.

➔ ____?

그 문제는 중요하니?

10. He is a baseball player.

➔ ____________________?

그는 야구 선수이니?

11. Mike is a picky eater.

➔ ____________________?

Mike는 입맛이 까다로운 사람이니?

12. You are late for school.

➔ ____?

너는 학교에 늦었니?

13. I am lazy.

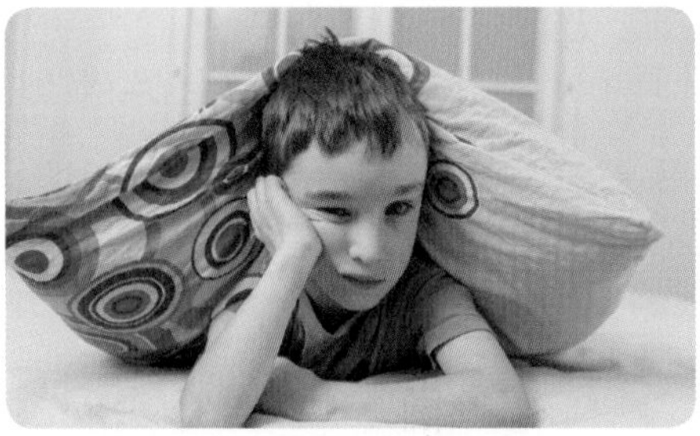

➔ ____________________?

나는 게으르니?

14. They are young.

➔ ____________________?

그들은 어리니?

정답과 해설 p.6

Let's Practice More!

SET 06

학습목표 3 | be동사의 의문문을 연습해 보아요. 공부한 날 : 맞은 개수 : /14개

다음 보기 와 같이 의문문에 대한 긍정적 대답과 부정적 대답을 완성해 보세요.

> 보기 Are you late? 너 늦었니?
>
> A: Yes, I am.
>
> B: No, I am not[I'm not].

01. Are they your friends?
그들은 너의 친구들이니?

A: Yes, they are.

B: No, they are not [they aren't/they're not].

02. Is it long?
그것은 길이가 기니?

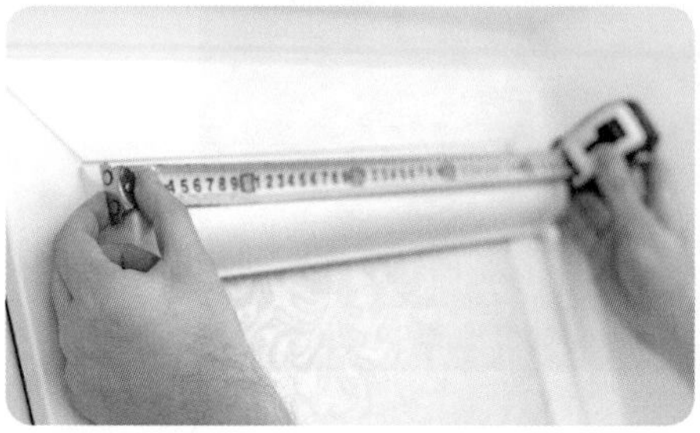

A: Yes, ______.

B: No, ______.

03. Are you a fan of Exo? 너는 엑소의 팬이니?

A: Yes, ______.

B: No, ______.

04. Is she kind? 그녀는 친절하니?

A: Yes, ______.

B: No, ______.

05. Are you thirsty? 너 목마르니?

A: Yes, ______.

B: No, ______.

정답과 해설 p.6

06. Is it easy? 그거 쉽니?
A: Yes, ________________________________.
B: No, ________________________________.

07. Are we late for school? 우리 학교에 늦었니?
A: Yes, ________________________________.
B: No, ________________________________.

08. Are they your parents? 그들은 너의 부모님이시니?
A: Yes, ________________________________.
B: No, ________________________________.

09. Is he weak? 그는 약하니?
A: Yes, ________________________________.
B: No, ________________________________.

10. Is she a good dancer? 그녀는 춤을 잘 추니?
A: Yes, ________________________________.
B: No, ________________________________.

11. Is her brother a student? 그녀의 오빠는 학생이니?
A: Yes, ________________________.
B: No, ________________________.

12. Are you sure? 넌 확신하니?
A: Yes, ________________________________.
B: No, ________________________________.

13. Are they tall? 그들은 키가 크니?
A: Yes, ________________________________.
B: No, ________________________________.

14. Is she a grown-up? 그녀는 어른이니?
A: Yes, ________________________________.
B: No, ________________________________.

정답과 해설 p.6

Let's Practice More!

SET 07

학습목표 4 | **be동사의 부정문과 의문문을 써 보아요.**　　공부한 날 :　　맞은 개수 :　　/20개

다음 주어진 문장을 부정문으로 바꿔 보세요.

01. The kitchen is clean.

➔ The kitchen is not[isn't] clean.

그 주방은 깨끗하지 않아.

02. The baby is awake.

➔ ______________________________.

그 아기는 깨어있지 않아.

03. Your dog is cute.

➔ ______________________________. 너의 개는 귀엽지 않아.

04. She is rich.

➔ ______________________________. 그녀는 부유하지 않아.

05. Hayul is a big eater.

➔ ______________________________. 하율이는 대식가가 아니야.

06. My father is a good singer.

➔ ______________________________. 나의 아빠는 노래를 잘 못 부르셔.

07. Irene is a smart girl.

➔ ______________________________. Irene은 똑똑한 소녀가 아니야.

08. We are sleepy.

➔ ______________________________. 우리는 졸리지 않아.

09. I am a fool.

➔ ______________________________. 나는 바보가 아니야.

정답과 해설 p.6

10. My mom is inside the house. 나의 엄마는 집 안에 계시지 않아.

➔ ______________________________.

11. They are tired.

➔ ______________________________

______________________________.

그들은 피곤하지 않아.

12. You are weak.

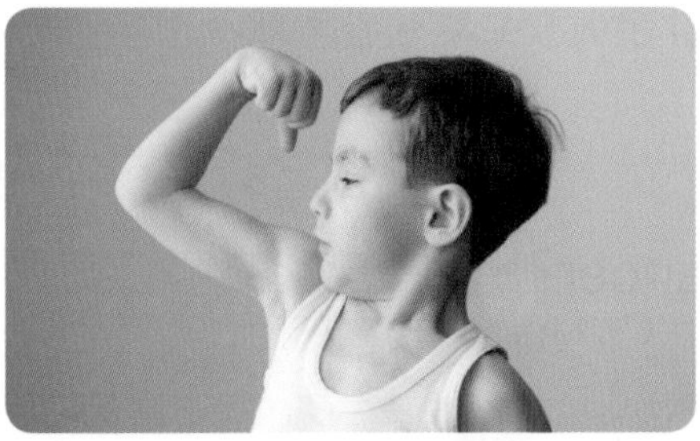

➔ ______________________________

______________________________.

너는 약하지 않아.

13. The problem is important.

➔ ______________________________. 그 문제는 중요하지 않아.

14. Our classroom is clean.

➔ ______________________________. 우리의 교실은 깨끗하지 않아.

15. The webtoon is funny.

➔ ______________________________. 그 웹툰은 재미있지 않아.

16. They are your real friends.

➔ ______________________________. 그들은 너의 진정한 친구들이 아니야.

17. She is afraid of birds.

➔ ______________________________. 그녀는 새를 두려워 하지 않아.

18. We are in the same class.

➔ ______________________________. 우리는 같은 반이 아니야.

19. My parents are in Seoul.

➔ ______________________________. 나의 부모님은 서울에 계시지 않아.

20. I am lazy.

➔ ______________________________. 나는 게으르지 않아.

정답과 해설 p.6

Let's Practice More!

SET 08

학습목표 4 | **be동사의 부정문과 의문문을 써 보아요.** 공부한 날 : 맞은 개수 : /20개

다음 우리말 뜻에 맞도록 빈칸을 채워 의문문과 부정문을 완성해 보세요.

01. __Is__ __she__ a good dancer? 그녀는 춤을 잘 추니?

02. They ________ ________ fat. 그들은 뚱뚱하지 않아.

03. He ________ ________ at home. 그는 집에 있지 않아.

04. They ________ ________ children anymore. 그들은 더 이상 어린애가 아니야.

05. ________ ________ tired? 너 피곤하니?

06. ________ ________ brother kind? 너의 오빠는 친절하니?

07. She ________ ________ mean. 그녀는 심술궂지 않아.

08. I ________ ________ your enemy. 나는 너의 적이 아니야.

09. ________ ________ a soccer player? 그는 축구선수니?

정답과 해설 p.6

10. We ___________ ___________ hungry. 우리는 배고프지 않아.

11. It ___________ ___________ easy. 그건 쉽지 않아.

12. ___________ ___________ your parents? 그들은 너의 부모님이시니?

13. It ___________ ___________ funny. 그것은 재밌지 않다.

14. ___________ ___________ angry? 너 화났니?

15. ___________ ___________ a teacher? 그녀는 선생님이니?

16. ___________ ___________ tall? 그들은 키가 크니?

17. I ___________ ___________ a picky eater. 난 입맛이 까다로운 사람이 아니야.

18. He ___________ ___________ my best friend. 그는 나의 가장 친한 친구가 아니다.

19. Sihu ___________ ___________ a good rapper. 시후는 랩을 잘 못한다.

20. ___________ ___________ thirsty? 너 목마르니?

정답과 해설 p.6

실전테스트

CHAPTER 01~02

공부한 날 :

복습한 날 :

부모님 확인 :

CHAPTER 01 일반동사 CHAPTER 02 be동사의 부정문과 의문문

● 정답과 해설은 별책 6쪽에서 확인하세요!!

01

다음 그림을 보고, 우리말 해석과 같도록 빈칸에 알맞은 말을 쓰세요.

She __________ __________ angry.
(그녀는 화가 나지 않았다.)

02

다음 그림과 단어가 바르게 짝지어지지 않은 것을 고르세요.

①

wash

②

watch

③

read

④

sleep

[03~06] 다음 문장의 밑줄 친 동사를 바르게 고친 것을 고르세요.

03

She have a nice bike.

① has ② haves
③ is ④ are

04

Mary wash her hands.

① wash ② washing
③ washes ④ was

05

My school bus pass here.

① passing ② not passing
③ passes ④ are

06

He try her carrot cake.

① trys ② is
③ does ④ tries

07

다음 그림과 단어가 바르게 짝지어지지 않은 것을 고르세요.

①

cut

②

bark

③

hide

④

change

[08~12] 다음 그림에 맞게 주어진 단어를 배열하여 문장을 완성하세요.

08

(cat, A, ice cream, eats).

⇨ ______________________________

09

(pretty, princess, The, is).

⇨ ______________________________

10

(love, animals, I).

⇨ ______________________________

11

(Jenny, shoes, red, likes).

⇨ ______________________________

12

(school, They, dance, at).

⇨ ______________________________

[13~14] 순서에 맞게 단어들을 배열하여 문장을 완성하세요.

13

(Are / from / you / China)?

⇨ ______________________________

14

(is / She / not / angry).

⇨ ______________________________

[15~16] 다음 그림을 보고 우리말과 뜻이 같도록 괄호 안의 동사를 바르게 바꿔 쓰세요.

15

She __________ the book. (read)

(그녀는 책을 읽는다.)

16

He __________ the boxes. (carry)

(그는 상자들을 나른다.)

17

다음 그림에 맞게 빈칸에 알맞은 말을 쓰세요.

A: Is she tired?

B: Yes, she __________.

18

다음 대화의 빈칸에 공통으로 들어갈 알맞은 단어를 고르세요.

A: __________ he your cousin?

B: Yes, he __________.

① Do[do] ② Does[does]

③ Are[are] ④ Is[is]

[19~21] 괄호 안의 단어 중 맞는 것에 ○표 하세요.

19

She (play / plays) the piano very well.

20

You (look / looks) good today.

21

They (like / likes) the book.

[22~23] 다음 그림과 일치하도록 빈칸에 알맞은 말을 쓰세요.

22

She ________ basketball.

23

She ________ to school.

[24~25] 다음 문장을 부정문으로 만들 때 not이 들어갈 자리를 고르세요.

24

She ① is ② a ③ child ④ .

____

25

He ① is ② in ③ the ④ cafe.

____

26

다음 그림을 참고하여 빈칸에 알맞은 말을 쓰세요.

A: ________ your sister tall?

(너의 여동생은 키가 크니?)

B: Yes, ________ ________.

(응, 키가 커.)

[27~28] 다음 단어들을 순서에 맞게 배열하여 문장을 완성하세요.

27

(has / She / breakfast / every day).

⇨ ________________________

28

(It / your / is / cat).

⇨ ________________________

[29~30] 다음 밑줄 친 부분을 바르게 고쳐 문장을 다시 쓰세요.

29

우리는 너를 좋아한다.

→ We <u>likes</u> you.

____

30

Tom은 빵을 먹는다.

→ Tom <u>eat</u> bread.

____

Chapter 03 일반동사의 부정문과 의문문

이 챕터에서는 일반동사의 부정문과 축약형,
그리고 일반동사의 의문문과 그에 대한 대답에 대해 배워 보아요.

☆ 학습 방향 및 배울 내용 미리보기 ☆

☐ **Unit 01 : I do not[don't] eat onions.**

일반동사의 부정문

일반동사의 부정문을 만드는 방법과 줄여 쓰는 방법에 대해 알아보아요.

▼

☐ **Unit 02 : Do you want some juice?**

일반동사의 의문문

일반동사의 의문문을 만드는 방법과 일반동사 의문문에 대답하는 방법에 대해 배워 보아요.

단어 미리보기

이 챕터에 나올 단어들 중 이미 알고 있는 단어가 있나요?
맞는 뜻을 골라 체크해 봐요.

날짜 :   이름 :   알고 있는 단어의 수 :   /24개

No.	아는 단어	단어	품사	알맞은 뜻에 체크 표시해 봐요.			
1	☑	onion	명사	양파	☑	마늘	☐
2	☐	know	동사	말하다	☐	알다	☐
3	☐	smile	동사	웃다	☐	화내다	☐
4	☐	lie	동사	거짓말하다	☐	믿다	☐
5	☐	bag	명사	필통	☐	가방	☐
6	☐	tooth	명사	혀	☐	이	☐
7	☐	homework	명사	숙제	☐	휴식	☐
8	☐	science	명사	수학	☐	과학	☐
9	☐	food	명사	물	☐	음식	☐
10	☐	basketball	명사	농구	☐	야구	☐
11	☐	walk	동사	일하다	☐	걷다	☐
12	☐	come	동사	돌다	☐	오다	☐
13	☐	sleep	동사	잠자다	☐	깨다	☐
14	☐	socks	명사	양말	☐	신발	☐
15	☐	wear	동사	입다	☐	벗다	☐
16	☐	summer	명사	겨울	☐	여름	☐
17	☐	kind	형용사	친절한	☐	나쁜	☐
18	☐	movie	명사	영화	☐	이사	☐
19	☐	birthday	명사	생일	☐	휴일	☐
20	☐	blue	형용사	파란	☐	노란	☐
21	☐	time	명사	시간	☐	시계	☐
22	☐	color	명사	목도리	☐	색	☐
23	☐	watch	동사	보다	☐	듣다	☐
24	☐	math	명사	수학	☐	과학	☐

UNIT 01 일반동사의 부정문

UNIT 01 I do not[don't] eat onions.

❖ POiNT ❖

일반동사의 부정문은 '~않다'라는 의미의 조동사 do not/does not을 쓰고 뒤에는 항상 일반동사 원형을 써요.

I	do not (=don't)
you	
we	
they	

I do not eat onions. 난 양파를 먹지 않아.
You do not have a cat. 너는 고양이를 갖고 있지 않아.
We don't talk anymore. 우리는 더 이상 이야기하지 않아.
They don't trust you. 그들은 너를 믿지 않아.

he	does not (=doesn't)
she	
it	

He does not text me. 그는 나에게 문자를 보내지 않아.
She doesn't know me. 그녀는 날 몰라.
It doesn't matter. 그건 중요하지 않아.

Check and Write

다음 빈칸에 알맞은 일반동사의 부정형을 쓰세요.

1. I [do not] hurt you.
   I [don't] hurt you.
   나는 너를 해치지 않아.

2. She [ ] smile.
   She [ ] smile.
   그녀는 웃지 않아.

3. They [ ] lie.
   They [ ] lie.
   그들은 거짓말하지 않아.

4. You [ ] talk.
   You [ ] talk.
   너는 말하지 않아.

5. It [ ] come out of the bag.
   It [ ] come out of the bag.
   그것은 그 가방에서 나오지 않아.

정답과 해설 p.7

UNIT

02 Do you want some juice?

일반동사의 의문문

❖ POiNT ❖

일반동사 의문문은 "Do[Does] + 주어 + 동사원형 ~ ?"의 순으로 써요.
대답은 "Yes, 주어 + do[does].", "No, 주어 + don't[doesn't]."로 해요.

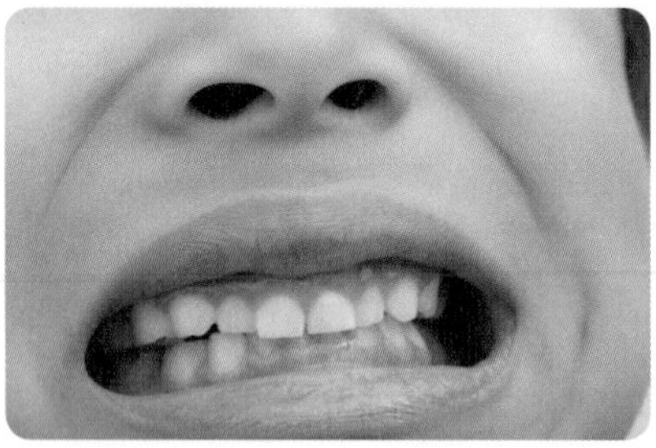

Do	I	동사원형 ~?
	you	
	we	
	they	

Do I have something in my teeth?
나 이에 뭐 꼈어?

Yes, you do. / No, you don't.
응, 꼈어. / 아니, 끼지 않았어.

Do you want some juice? 너 주스 좀 원하니?
Yes, I do. / No, I don't.
응, 원해. / 아니, 원하지 않아.

Do we have homework? 우리 숙제 있어?
Yes, we do. / No, we don't.
응, 있어. / 아니, 없어.

Do they need a break? 걔네들은 휴식이 필요해?
Yes, they do. / No, they don't.
응, 필요해. / 아니, 필요하지 않아.

Does	he	동사원형 ~?
	she	
	it	

Does he like me? 그가 날 좋아해?
Yes, he does. / No, he doesn't.
응, 좋아해. / 아니, 좋아하지 않아.

Does she have a brother?
그녀는 오빠(남동생)가 있니?

Yes, she does. / No, she doesn't.
응, 있어. / 아니, 없어.

Does it work? 그거 효과 있어?
Yes, it does. / No, it doesn't.
응, 있어. / 아니, 없어.

Check and Write

빈칸을 채워 의문문과 답변을 완성해 보세요.

1. [Do] you like Honey Butter Chip?
너는 허니버터칩을 좋아하니?
– Yes, I [do]. 응, 좋아해.
– No, I [don't]. 아니, 좋아하지 않아.

2. [　　] she have homework?
그녀는 숙제가 있니?
– Yes, she [　　]. 응, 있어.
– No, she [　　]. 아니, 없어.

3. [　　] you need a break?
너는 휴식이 필요하니?
– Yes, I [　　]. 응, 필요해.
– No, I [　　]. 아니, 필요하지 않아.

4. [　　] he have a brother?
그는 형제가 있니?
– Yes, he [　　]. 응, 있어.
– No, he [　　]. 아니, 없어.

5. [　　] they have a party?
그들은 파티를 하니?
– Yes, they [　　]. 응, 해.
– No, they [　　]. 아니, 하지 않아.

정답과 해설 p.7

Practice 1 일반동사가 쓰인 문장의 부정문과 의문문을 익혀 보아요.

우리말 해석과 같은 뜻이 되도록 빈칸에 들어갈 알맞은 표현을 보기 에서 골라 쓰세요. (중복 사용 가능)

보기 Do[do] don't Does[does] doesn't

A At school

1. *Joey*: __Do__ we have a science test today?
   우리 오늘 과학 시험 있니?
   Mina: No, we __don't__. 아니, 없어.

2. *Joey*: ________ Zico release his new single today?
   지코가 오늘 새로운 싱글을 발표하니? (*release: 발표하다, 발매하다)
   Nari: Yes, he ________. 응, 발표해.

3. *Joey*: ________ your sister share food with you?
   네 여동생은 너와 음식을 나누어 먹니?
   Sihu: Yes, she ________. 응, 나누어 먹어.

4. *Mina*: ________ you eat vegetables? 너 야채를 먹니?
   Joey: No, I ________. 아니, 먹지 않아.

5. *Joey*: ________ Kevin play basketball with Sam?
   Kevin은 Sam과 농구를 하니?
   Sihu: No, he ________. 아니, 하지 않아.

B After school

1. *Joey*: Look at that cat. ________ you like cats?
   저 고양이 좀 봐. 너 고양이 좋아하니?
   Amy: Yes, I ________. 응, 좋아해.

정답과 해설 p.7

2. *Joey*: ___________ you drink a lot of water? 너 물 많이 마시니?

Amy: Yes, I ___________. 응, 많이 마셔.

3. *Amy*: ___________ your father play badminton?

너의 아버지는 배드민턴을 치시니?

Joey: No, he ___________. 아니, 안 치셔.

4. *Amy*: ___________ pigeons walk fast? (*pigeon: 비둘기)

비둘기는 빨리 걷니?

Joey: Yes, they ___________. 응, 빨리 걸어.

C Joey talks with her mom.

1. *Mom*: ___________ your friends' parents come to school today?

너의 친구들 부모님은 오늘 학교에 오시니?

Joey: No, they ___________. 아니요, 오지 않으세요.

2. *Mom*: ___________ students like the lunch menu?

학생들이 점심 메뉴를 좋아하니?

Joey: No, they ___________. 아니요, 좋아하지 않아요.

3. *Mom*: ___________ your friends go to the cyber cafe? (*cyber cafe: PC방)

너의 친구들은 PC방에 가니?

Joey: No, they ___________. 아니요, 가지 않아요.

4. *Mom*: ___________ your friends play baseball after school?

너의 친구들은 방과 후에 야구 하니?

Joey: Yes, they ___________. 네, 해요.

정답과 해설 p.7

D Joey talks about herself and her friends.

1. I __________ have time to sleep.
   나는 잘 시간이 없다.

2. I __________ wear socks in summer.
   나는 여름에는 양말을 신지 않는다.

3. Nari is not kind. She __________ care about other people. (*care about: ~에 대해 신경을 쓰다)
   나리는 친절하지 않다. 그녀는 다른 사람들에 대해 신경 쓰지 않는다.

4. People __________ like the movie, "Batman vs. Superman."
   사람들은 영화 '배트맨 대 슈퍼맨'을 좋아하지 않는다.

5. I __________ remember my brother's birthday.
   난 우리 오빠의 생일을 기억하지 못한다.

6. __________ they take pictures?
   그들은 사진을 찍니?

7. Eric __________ watch TV shows.
   Eric은 TV 쇼를 보지 않는다.

정답과 해설 p.7

Practice 2 표현을 알맞게 배열해서 일반동사가 쓰인 문장의 부정문과 의문문을 완성해 보아요.

다음 주어진 우리말 해석에 맞게 영어 표현을 배열하여 문장을 완성하세요.

1. (Do, walk fast, ducks)?

오리가 빨리 걷니?

➔ Do ducks walk fast ?

2. (eat, fish, Do, you)?

너희는 생선을 먹니?

➔ ______________________?

3. (the movie, don't, People, like), "The Jungle Book."

사람들은 '정글북' 영화를 좋아하지 않는다.

➔ ______________________, "The Jungle Book."

4. (like, club activities, Do, students)?

학생들은 동아리 활동을 좋아하니?

➔ ______________________?

5. (your dog, Does, jump high)?

너의 개는 높이 점프하니?

➔ ______________________?

6. (have an English test, Do, we) today?

우리 오늘 영어 시험을 보니?

➔ ______________________ today?

정답과 해설 p.7

7. (you, take a walk, Do) with your dog?
너는 너의 개와 함께 산책을 하니?

➜ ______________________________ with your dog?

8. (time, have, I, don't).
나는 시간이 없다.

➜ ____.

9. Jiwoo (like, bananas, doesn't).
지우는 바나나를 좋아하지 않는다.

➜ Jiwoo ______________.

10. (Jane, study, with Karen, Does)? Jane은 Karen과 함께 공부하니?

➜ __________________?

11. (wear, I, don't, a muffler) in winter.
나는 겨울에 목도리를 하지 않는다.

➜ ______________________________ in winter.

12. (doesn't, care about, He) other people.
그는 다른 사람들에 대해 신경 쓰지 않는다.

➜ ______________________________ other people.

13. (Karen's birthday, remember, don't, I).
나는 Karen의 생일이 기억나지 않는다.

➜ ____.

정답과 해설 p.7

14. (don't, take notes, Students) in their books.
학생들은 책에 필기를 하지 않는다. (*take notes: **필기하다**)

➔ ______________________________ in their books.

15. (don't, go, They) to the mall.
그들은 쇼핑몰에 가지 않는다.

➔ ______________________________ to the mall.

16. (come, your parents, Do) to school?
너의 부모님은 학교에 오시니?

➔ ______________________________ to school?

17. (play games, I, Do) a lot?
내가 게임을 많이 하니?

➔ ______________ a lot?

18. (the color blue, like, you, Do)?
너는 파란색을 좋아하니?

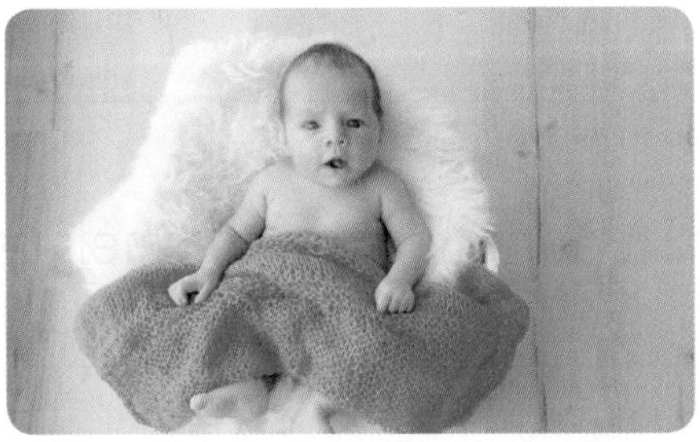

➔ ______________?

19. (play baseball, your friends, Do) after school?
너의 친구들은 방과 후에 야구를 하니?

➔ ______________________________ after school?

Practice 3 일반동사의 부정문과 의문문을 써 보아요.

우리말 해석을 참고하여 주어진 표현을 사용해 문장을 영어로 완성해 보세요.

1. (fight with, every day)

Jake는 Mark와 매일 싸우니?

→ Does Jake fight with Mark every day ?

2. (your friends, go to the library)

너의 친구들은 도서관에 가니?

→ ______________________ ______________________?

3. (eat, breakfast) 나는 아침밥을 먹지 않는다.

→ ______________________.

4. (care about) Sam은 그의 건강에 대해 신경 쓰지 않는다.

→ ______________________ his health.

5. (remember, his phone number) 나는 그의 전화번호가 기억나지 않는다.

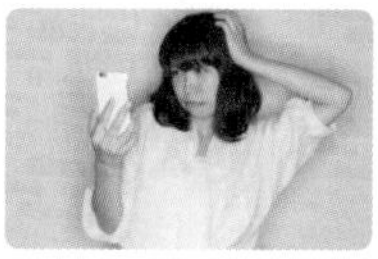

→ ______________________.

6. (Students, listen to, their teacher) 학생들은 선생님의 말을 듣지 않는다.

→ ______________________.

7. (Mina, like) 미나는 액션 영화를 좋아하지 않는다.

→ ______________________ action movies.

8. (Children, like, sad movies) 아이들은 슬픈 영화를 좋아하지 않는다.

→ ______________________.

9. (your computer, make noise) 너의 컴퓨터는 소음을 내니?

→ ______________________?

정답과 해설 p.7

10. (turtles, swim fast)

거북이가 빨리 헤엄치니?

➔ ______________________________?

11. (eat, beans)

너는 콩을 먹니?

➔ ______________________________?

12. (wear, a watch) 나는 손목시계를 차지 않는다.

➔ ____.

13. (have, a math class) 오늘 우리 수학 수업이 있니?

➔ ______________________________ today?

14. (your sister, share clothes) 너의 언니는 너와 옷을 같이 입니?

➔ ______________________________ with you?

15. (like, movies) 나는 영화를 좋아하지 않는다.

➔ ____.

16. (go to church) 그들은 교회에 가지 않는다.

➔ ____.

17. (like, the color violet) 너는 보라색을 좋아하니?

➔ ______________________________________?

18. (your friends, eat snacks) 너의 친구들은 방과 후에 간식을 먹니?

➔ ______________________________ after school?

19. (Jane, like, jelly) Jane은 젤리를 좋아하니?

➔ ____?

정답과 해설 p.7

Let's Practice More!

SET 01

학습목표 1 | 일반동사의 부정문 형태를 연습해 보아요. 공부한 날 : 맞은 개수 : /12개

다음 문장을 읽고 밑줄 친 부분이 맞으면 ○표, 틀리면 ×표를 하세요.

01. I do not have time to sleep. 나는 잘 시간이 없다. → ○

02. She do not care about other people. 그녀는 다른 사람들에 대해 신경 쓰지 않는다. → _____

03. I does not remember my brother's birthday. 난 우리 오빠의 생일을 기억하지 못한다. → _____

04. Eric does not watch TV shows. Eric은 TV 쇼를 보지 않는다. → _____

05. I do not have an umbrella. 나는 우산이 없어. → _____

06. Students do not take notes in their books. 학생들은 책에 필기를 하지 않는다. → _____

07. Jiwoo do not like bananas. 지우는 바나나를 좋아하지 않는다. → _____

08. They does not go to the mall. 그들은 쇼핑몰에 가지 않는다. → _____

09. Sam do not care about his health. Sam은 그의 건강에 대해 신경 쓰지 않는다. → _____

10. Children do not like sad movies. 아이들은 슬픈 영화를 좋아하지 않는다. → _____

11. I do not wear a watch. 나는 손목시계를 차지 않는다. → _____

12. They does not go to church. 그들은 교회에 가지 않는다. → _____

정답과 해설 p.7

Let's Practice More!

SET 02

학습목표 1 | 일반동사의 부정문 형태를 연습해 보아요. 공부한 날 : 맞은 개수 : /14개

다음 ( ) 안에서 알맞은 것을 골라 보세요.

01. I (do not / does not) eat breakfast. 나는 아침밥을 먹지 않는다.

02. They (do not / does not) trust you. 그들은 너를 믿지 않아.

03. She (do not / does not) remember her brother's birthday.
그녀는 그녀의 오빠의 생일을 기억하지 못한다.

04. I (do not / does not) have time to sleep. 나는 잘 시간이 없다.

05. I (do not / does not) wear socks in summer. 나는 여름에는 양말을 신지 않는다.

06. People (do not / does not) like the movie, "Batman vs. Superman."
사람들은 영화 '배트맨 대 슈퍼맨'을 좋아하지 않는다.

07. I (do not / does not) wear a muffler in winter.
나는 겨울에 목도리를 하지 않는다.

08. He (do not / does not) care about other people.
그는 다른 사람들에 대해 신경 쓰지 않는다.

09. I (do not / does not) like horror movies.
나는 공포 영화를 좋아하지 않는다.

10. Mina (do not / does not) like action movies.
미나는 액션 영화를 좋아하지 않는다.

11. I (do not / does not) remember Karen's birthday.
나는 Karen의 생일이 기억나지 않는다.

12. She (do not / does not) remember his phone number.
그녀는 그의 전화번호가 기억나지 않는다.

13. Students (do not / does not) listen to their teachers.
학생들은 선생님의 말을 듣지 않는다.

14. Karen (do not / does not) go to church.
Karen은 교회에 가지 않는다.

정답과 해설 p.7

Let's Practice More!

SET 03

학습목표 2 | 일반동사의 부정문은 주어에 따라 모양이 바뀌어요. 공부한 날 : 맞은 개수 : /14개

밑줄 친 부분이 맞으면 ○표, 틀리면 고쳐 써 보세요.

01. I <u>don't</u> eat breakfast. → ○
나는 아침밥을 먹지 않는다.

02. Sam <u>don't</u> care about his health. → ______
Sam은 그의 건강에 대해 신경 쓰지 않는다.

03. I <u>doesn't</u> remember his phone number. → ______
나는 그의 전화번호가 기억나지 않는다.

04. Students <u>doesn't</u> listen to their teachers. → ______
학생들은 선생님의 말을 듣지 않는다.

05. Children <u>don't</u> like sad movies. 아이들은 슬픈 영화를 좋아하지 않는다. → ______

06. I <u>don't</u> wear a watch. 나는 손목시계를 차지 않는다. → ______

07. They <u>doesn't</u> trust you. 그들은 너를 믿지 않아. → ______

08. I <u>don't</u> have time to sleep. 나는 잘 시간이 없다. → ______

09. He <u>doesn't</u> wear socks in summer. 그는 여름에는 양말을 신지 않는다. → ______

10. I <u>doesn't</u> care about other people. 나는 다른 사람들에 대해 신경 쓰지 않는다. → ______

11. Eric <u>don't</u> watch TV shows. Eric은 TV 쇼를 보지 않는다. → ______

12. She <u>don't</u> wear a muffler in winter. 그녀는 겨울에 목도리를 하지 않는다. → ______

13. Students <u>don't</u> take notes in their books. 학생들은 책에 필기를 하지 않는다. → ______

14. Jisoo <u>don't</u> like bananas. 지수는 바나나를 좋아하지 않는다. → ______

정답과 해설 p.7

Let's Practice More!

SET 04

학습목표 3 | 일반동사의 의문문을 연습해 보아요. 공부한 날 : 맞은 개수 : /14개

우리말 해석과 같은 뜻이 되도록 다음 빈칸을 채워 보세요.

01. ___Do___ we have a science test today? 우리 오늘 과학 시험 있니?

02. ________ your sister share food with you? 네 여동생은 너와 음식을 나누어 먹니?

03. ________ you eat vegetables? 너 야채를 먹니?

04. ________ Kevin play basketball with Sam? Kevin은 Sam과 농구를 하니?

05. ________ you like cats? 너 고양이 좋아하니?

06. ________ students like the lunch menu? 학생들이 점심 메뉴를 좋아하니?

07. ________ your friends go to the cyber cafe? 너의 친구들은 PC방에 가니?

08. ________ Jack study with Ben? Jack은 Ben과 함께 공부하니?

09. ________ your parents come to school? 너의 부모님은 학교에 오시니?

10. ________ your computer make noise? 너의 컴퓨터는 소음을 내니?

11. ________ your sister share clothes with you? 너의 언니는 너와 옷을 같이 입니?

12. ________ your friends go to the library? 너의 친구들은 도서관에 가니?

13. ________ Jane like jelly? Jane은 젤리를 좋아하니?

14. ________ your dog jump high? 너의 개는 높이 점프하니?

정답과 해설 p.7

Let's Practice More!

SET 05

학습목표 3 | **일반동사의 의문문을 연습해 보아요.** 공부한 날 : 맞은 개수 : /14개

다음 문장을 의문문으로 바꾸어 쓰세요.

01. They take pictures.

➔ Do they take pictures

____________________?

그들은 사진을 찍니?

02. Your father plays badminton.

➔ ____________________

____________________?

너의 아버지는 배드민턴을 치시니?

03. Pigeons walk fast.

➔ ____?

비둘기는 빨리 걷니?

04. Your parents come to school.

➔ ____?

너의 부모님은 학교에 오시니?

05. Your friends play baseball.

➔ ____?

너의 친구들은 야구하니?

06. People like the movie, "Batman vs. Superman."

➔ ____?

사람들은 영화 '배트맨 대 슈퍼맨'을 좋아하니?

정답과 해설 p.8

07. You drink a lot of water.

➔ ____?

너 물 많이 마시니?

08. Your dog jumps high.

➔ ____?

너의 개는 높이 점프하니?

09. Jack studies with Ben.

➔ ____?

Jack은 Ben과 함께 공부하니?

10. Your friends play soccer after school.

➔ ____?

너의 친구들은 방과 후에 축구를 하니?

11. Mina likes action movies.

➔ ____?

미나는 액션 영화를 좋아하니?

12. Turtles swim fast.

➔ ____?

거북이가 빨리 헤엄치니?

13. Your computer makes noise.

➔ ____?

너의 컴퓨터는 소음을 내니?

14. We have a math class today.

➔ ____?

오늘 우리 수학 수업이 있니?

정답과 해설 p.8

Let's Practice More!

SET 06

학습목표 4 | 일반동사의 의문문에 대한 대답을 연습해 보아요.　　공부한 날 :　　맞은 개수 :　　/14개

다음 문장을 읽고 빈칸에 적절한 대답을 써보세요.

01.

Does your sister share food with you? 네 여동생은 너와 음식을 나누어 먹니?

– Yes, ___she___ ___does___.
응, 나누어 먹어.

– No, ___she___ ___doesn't___.
아니, 나누어 먹지 않아.

02.

Does Jake fight with Mark every day? Jake는 Mark와 매일 싸우니?

– Yes, ________ ________.
응, 매일 싸워.

– No, ________ ________.
아니, 매일 싸우지 않아.

03. Do we have a science test today? 우리 오늘 과학 시험 있니?

– Yes, ________ ________. 응, 있어.

– No, ________ ________. 아니, 없어.

04. Do you eat vegetables? 너(희)는 야채를 먹니?

– Yes, ________ ________. 응, 먹어.

– No, ________ ________. 아니, 먹지 않아.

05. Does Kevin play basketball with Sam? Kevin은 Sam과 농구를 하니?

– Yes, ________ ________. 응, 해.

– No, ________ ________. 아니, 하지 않아.

06. Do you like cats? 너(희) 고양이 좋아하니?

– Yes, ________ ________. 응, 좋아해.

– No, ________ ________. 아니, 좋아하지 않아.

정답과 해설 p.8

07. Do you drink a lot of water? 너(희) 물 많이 마시니?

– Yes, ___________ ___________. 응, 많이 마셔.

– No, ___________ ___________. 아니, 많이 마시지 않아.

08. Does your father play badminton? 너의 아버지는 배드민턴을 치시니?

– Yes, ___________ ___________. 응, 치셔.

– No, ___________ ___________. 아니, 안 치셔.

CH 03

09. Does your sister share clothes with you? 너의 언니는 너와 옷을 같이 입니?

– Yes, ___________ ___________. 응, 같이 입어.

– No, ___________ ___________. 아니, 같이 입지 않아.

10. Do students like club activities? 학생들은 동아리 활동을 좋아하니?

– Yes, ___________ ___________. 응, 좋아해.

– No, ___________ ___________. 아니, 좋아하지 않아.

11. Do ducks walk fast? 오리가 빨리 걷니?

– Yes, ___________ ___________. 응, 빨리 걸어.

– No, ___________ ___________. 아니, 빨리 걷지 않아.

12. Does Jane like jelly? Jane은 젤리를 좋아하니?

– Yes, ___________ ___________. 응, 좋아해.

– No, ___________ ___________. 아니, 좋아하지 않아.

13. Do you like the color blue? 너(희)는 파란색을 좋아하니?

– Yes, ___________ ___________. 응, 좋아해.

– No, ___________ ___________. 아니, 좋아하지 않아.

14. Do I play games a lot? 내가 게임을 많이 하니?

– Yes, ___________ ___________. 응, 많이 해.

– No, ___________ ___________. 아니, 많이 하지 않아.

정답과 해설 p.8

Let's Practice More!

SET 07

학습목표 5 | 일반동사의 부정문과 의문문 만드는 방법을 확실히 다져보아요. 공부한 날 : 맞은 개수 : /20개

( ) 안의 지시에 따라 문장을 바꿔 보세요.

01. 

Pigeons walk fast. (의문문)

➔ Do pigeons walk fast ?

비둘기는 빨리 걷니?

02. 

You eat fish. (부정문)

➔ ______________________.

너는 생선을 먹지 않는다.

03. Your parents come to school. (부정문)

➔ ______________________.

너의 부모님은 학교에 오시지 않는다.

04. Students like the lunch menu. (의문문)

➔ ______________________?

학생들이 점심 메뉴를 좋아하니?

05. Your friends go to the cyber cafe. (의문문)

➔ ______________________?

너의 친구들은 PC방에 가니?

06. Your friends play baseball. (의문문)

➔ ______________________?

너의 친구들은 야구하니?

07. He cares about other people. (의문문)

➔ ______________________?

그는 다른 사람들에 대해 신경 쓰니?

08. Jake fights with Mark every day. (부정문)

➔ ______________________.

Jake는 Mark와 매일 싸우지 않는다.

09. You go to the library. (의문문)

➔ ______________________?

너는 도서관에 가니?

정답과 해설 p.8

10. You want some juice. (부정문)

➜ ____.

너는 주스를 원하지 않는다.

11. They take pictures. (의문문)

➜ ____?

그들은 사진을 찍니?

12. Students like club activities. (부정문)

➜ ____.

학생들은 동아리 활동을 좋아하지 않는다.

13. Your dog jumps high. (의문문)

➜ ______________________________________?

너의 개는 높이 점프하니?

14. Mina likes action movies. (의문문)

➜ ____?

미나는 액션 영화를 좋아하니?

15. Ducks walk fast. (의문문)

➜ ____?

오리가 빨리 걷니?

16. Your computer makes noise. (부정문)

➜ ____.

너의 컴퓨터는 소음을 내지 않는다.

17. Jane likes jelly. (의문문)

➜ ____?

Jane은 젤리를 좋아하니?

18. We have an English test today. (의문문)

➜ ____?

우리 오늘 영어 시험을 보니?

19. Sam cares about his health. (의문문)

➜ ____?

Sam은 그의 건강에 대해 신경 쓰니?

20. You take a walk with your dog. (부정문)

➜ ______________________________________.

너는 너의 개와 함께 산책을 하지 않는다.

정답과 해설 p.8

Let's Practice More!

SET 08

학습목표 5 | 일반동사의 부정문과 의문문 만드는 방법을 확실히 다져보아요. 공부한 날 : 맞은 개수 : /20개

다음 우리말 해석에 맞도록 빈칸을 채워 문장을 완성해 보세요.

01. 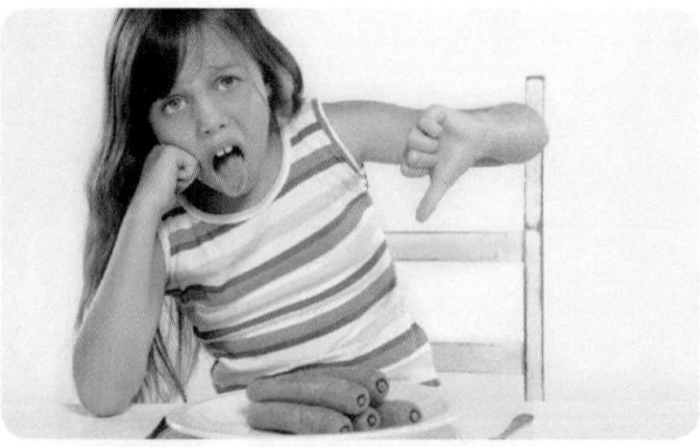

You ___do___ ___not___ eat carrot.

너는 당근을 먹지 않아.

02. 

He ________ ________ care about other people.

그는 다른 사람들에 대해 신경 쓰지 않아.

03. ________ we have an English test today? 우리 오늘 영어 시험을 보니?

04. You ________ ________ take a walk with your dog.

너는 너의 개와 함께 산책을 하지 않아.

05. I ________ ________ have time. 나는 시간이 없어.

06. ________ you remember Karen's birthday? 넌 Karen의 생일을 기억하니?

07. ________ Jiwoo like bananas? 지우는 바나나를 좋아하니?

08. You ________ like the color blue. 너는 파란색을 좋아하지 않아.

09. Mina ________ like action movies. 미나는 액션 영화를 좋아하지 않아.

정답과 해설 p.8

10. __________ your brother play games a lot?
너의 남동생은 게임을 많이 하니?

11. They __________ go to the mall. 그들은 쇼핑몰에 가지 않아.

12. Your parents __________ come to school. 너의 부모님은 학교에 오시지 않아.

13. Your sister __________ __________ share clothes with you.
너의 언니는 너와 옷을 같이 입지 않아.

14. 

__________ your friends play soccer after school?
너의 친구들은 방과 후에 축구를 하니?

15. 

Turtles __________ __________ walk fast.
거북이는 빨리 걷지 않아.

16. I __________ like movies. 나는 영화를 좋아하지 않아.

17. Kevin __________ play basketball with Sam. Kevin은 Sam과 농구를 하지 않아.

18. Your father __________ __________ play badminton. 너의 아버지는 배드민턴을 치시지 않아.

19. They __________ trust you. 그들은 너를 믿지 않아.

20. Children __________ like sad movies. 아이들은 슬픈 영화를 좋아하지 않아.

정답과 해설 p.8

Chapter 04 의문사 의문문

이 챕터에서는 의문사 who, what, when, where, how, why가 쓰인
'의문사 의문문'에 대해 배워 보아요.

☆ 학습 방향 및 배울 내용 미리보기 ☆

☐ Unit 01 : What is it? It is a Nintendo.

의문사가 있는 의문문 만드는 법

문장에서 be동사가 쓰였을 때와 일반동사가 쓰였을 때 의문문을 만드는 방법을 알려 줄게요.

▼

☐ Unit 02 : Who is she?

who/what 의문문

의문사 who가 쓰인 who 의문문과 의문사 what이 쓰인 what 의문문에 대해 알아보아요.

▼

☐ Unit 03 : When is your birthday?

when/where 의문문

의문사 when이 쓰인 when 의문문과 의문사 where가 쓰인 where 의문문에 대해 알아보아요.

▼

☐ Unit 04 : Why are you sad?

how/why 의문문

의문사 how가 쓰인 how 의문문과 의문사 why가 쓰인 why 의문문에 대해 알아보아요.

단어 미리보기

이 챕터에 나올 단어들 중 이미 알고 있는 단어가 있나요?
맞는 뜻을 골라 체크해 봐요.

날짜 : 이름 : 알고 있는 단어의 수 : /24개

No.	아는 단어	단어	품사	알맞은 뜻에 체크 표시해 봐요.			
1	☑	head	명사	머리	☑	손	☐
2	☐	place	명사	놀이터	☐	장소	☐
3	☐	new	형용사	낡은	☐	새로운	☐
4	☐	say	동사	노래하다	☐	말하다	☐
5	☐	read	동사	읽다	☐	보다	☐
6	☐	book	명사	책	☐	책상	☐
7	☐	vacation	명사	숙제	☐	휴가	☐
8	☐	buy	동사	사다	☐	저금하다	☐
9	☐	afternoon	명사	아침	☐	오후	☐
10	☐	sunny	형용사	비 오는	☐	화창한	☐
11	☐	sick	형용사	건강한	☐	아픈	☐
12	☐	school	명사	학교	☐	학원	☐
13	☐	bicycle	명사	오토바이	☐	자전거	☐
14	☐	today	명사	어제	☐	오늘	☐
15	☐	rainy	형용사	비가 오는	☐	맑은	☐
16	☐	umbrella	명사	지팡이	☐	우산	☐
17	☐	playground	명사	수영장	☐	운동장	☐
18	☐	find	동사	보다	☐	찾다	☐
19	☐	hair	명사	머리카락	☐	머리	☐
20	☐	late	형용사	늦은	☐	빠른	☐
21	☐	door	명사	유리	☐	문	☐
22	☐	busy	형용사	바쁜	☐	한가한	☐
23	☐	bookstore	명사	약국	☐	서점	☐
24	☐	people	명사	강아지	☐	사람들	☐

의문사가 있는 의문문 만드는 법

UNIT 01 What is it? It is a Nintendo.

의문사가 있는 의문문을 만드는 방법은 문장에서 be동사가 쓰였느냐, 일반동사가 쓰였느냐에 따라 달라요!

❖ POiNT 1 ❖

be동사의 의문문 만드는 법 기억하죠?

be동사가 쓰였을 때는 be동사의 의문문 앞에 의문사(who, what, when, where, how, why)만 붙여주면 돼요!

〈의문사+be동사+주어~?〉

평서문		It is	a Nintendo.	그것은 닌텐도야.
be동사 의문문		Is it	a Nintendo?	그거 닌텐도야?
의문사 의문문	What	is it?		그것은 무엇이니?

❖ POiNT 2 ❖

일반동사의 의문문 만드는 법 기억하나요?

일반동사가 쓰였을 때는 일반동사의 의문문 앞에 의문사(who, what, when, where, how, why)를 붙여주면 돼요!

〈의문사+do[does, did]+주어+동사원형~?〉

평서문		You want	a toy.	너는 장난감을 원한다.
일반동사 의문문		Do you want	a toy?	너는 장난감을 원하니?
의문사 의문문	What	do you want?		너는 무엇을 원하니?

Check and Write

다음 주어진 단어들을 순서에 맞게 나열해서 문장을 완성해 보세요.

1. What | want | he | does ?

What does he want ?

그는 무엇을 원하니?

2. do | When | leave | you ?

______ ?

너는 언제 떠나니?

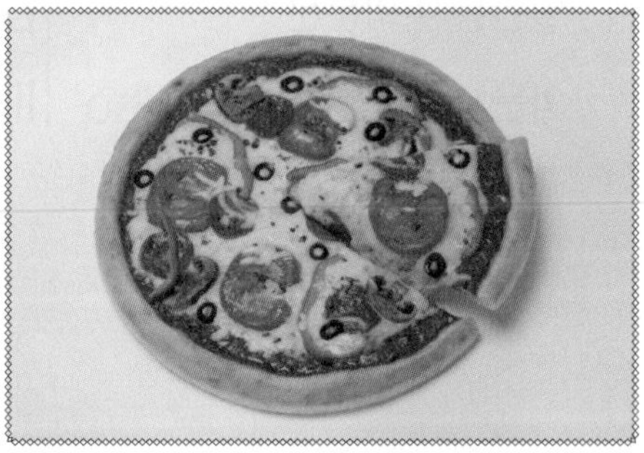

3. is | your favorite food | What ?

______ ?

네가 가장 좋아하는 음식은 무엇이니?

4. meet | Who | you | do ?

______ ?

너는 누구를 만나니?

5. Where | you | do | go ?

______ ?

너는 어디에 가니?

정답과 해설 p.8

UNIT

02 Who is she?

who/what 의문문

❖ POiNT 1 ❖

Who란 '누가/누구를' 이라는 뜻을 가진 의문사예요.

Sihu : Who is she? 그녀는 누구야?

Mina: She is my friend. 그녀는 내 친구야.

평서문		He meets	Mina.	그는 미나를 만난다.
일반동사 의문문		Does he meet	Mina?	그는 미나를 만나니?
의문사 의문문	Who	does he meet?		그는 누구를 만나니?

평서문		Mina likes	Sihu.	미나가 시후를 좋아해.
일반동사 의문문		Does Mina like	Sihu?	미나가 시후를 좋아해?
의문사 의문문	Who	likes Sihu?		누가 시후를 좋아해?

❖ POiNT 2 ❖

What이란 '무엇' 이라는 뜻을 가진 의문사예요. 이에 대한 대답은 일이나 사건, 사물로 해요.

Sihu : What is this? 이거 뭐야?

Mina: This is a blueberry cake. 이건 블루베리 케이크야.

평서문		It is	a present.	그것은 선물이야.
be동사 의문문		Is it	a present?	그것은 선물이야?
의문사 의문문	What	is it?		그것은 무엇이니?

Check and Write

다음 빈칸에 알맞은 의문사를 넣어 보세요.

1. [Who] is that girl?
저 여자애는 누구야?

2. [ ] is your name?
너의 이름이 무엇이니?

3. [ ] is your sister?
누가 너의 언니야?

4. [ ] do you like?
너는 무엇을 좋아하니?

5. [ ] likes cooking?
누가 요리하는 것을 좋아하니?

6. [ ] does she study?
그녀는 무엇을 공부하니?

정답과 해설 p.9

Practice 1 의문사가 있는 의문문을 익혀 보아요.

다음 문장에 알맞은 단어를 보기에서 골라 빈칸에 써 보세요. (중복 사용 가능)

A Just wondering

보기 What Who

1. ___What___ do you want for your birthday?
너는 생일 선물로 무엇을 원하니?

2. ________ do you need? 너는 무엇이 필요하니?

3. ________ is your favorite game? (*favorite: 가장 좋아하는)
네가 가장 좋아하는 게임은 뭐야?

4. ________ do you meet? 너는 누구를 만나니?

5. ________ do you like? 넌 누구를 좋아해?

B What's your hobby?

보기 What is Who does are

1. ________ do you like? 너는 무엇을 좋아하니?

2. ________ wants to see a movie?
누가 영화를 보고 싶니?

3. What ________ your hobby? (*hobby: 취미) 넌 취미가 뭐니?

4. What ________ you doing tonight? 너 오늘 밤에 뭐 할 거야?

5. What ________ she do in winter? 그녀는 겨울에 무엇을 하니?

정답과 해설 p.9

C What happened at dinner?

보기 Who do is What

1. Mom, what __________ we have for dinner?
엄마, 우리 저녁으로 뭘 먹어요?

2. __________ skips dinner? (*skip: 건너뛰다) 누가 저녁을 거르니?

3. What __________ that smell?
저 냄새 뭐야? (무슨 냄새야?)

4. __________ helps me? 누가 나를 도와줄 거야?

5. __________ can I do for you? 제가 무엇을 해 드릴 수 있을까요?

D Who?

보기 do does wakes says is

1. Who __________ that girl? 저 여자애는 누구야?

2. Who __________ so? 누가 그렇게 말해?

3. Who __________ you up? (*wake up: ~을 깨우다) 누가 너를 깨워줘?

4. Who __________ she play with?
그녀는 누구와 함께 놀아?

5. Who __________ you dislike? 너는 누구를 싫어하니?

정답과 해설 p.9

Practice 2 의문사가 있는 의문문을 완성해 보아요.

다음 우리말 뜻과 같도록 주어진 영어 표현을 순서에 맞게 배열하여 문장을 완성하세요.

1. (is, that little boy, Who)?
저 어린 남자애는 누구야?

→ Who is that little boy ?

2. (What, her name, is)?
그녀의 이름은 무엇이니?

→ ____________________?

3. *A*: (that woman, Who, is)? 저 여자 분은 누구니?
B: She is my mom. 우리 엄마이셔.
→ *A*: ____________________?
B: She is my mom.

4. *A*: (that, What, is) on your desk? 네 책상 위에 있는 저건 뭐야?
B: It is a letter. 그건 편지야.
→ *A*: ____________________ on your desk?
B: It is a letter.

5. *A*: (are, those people, Who)? 저 사람들은 누구니?
B: They are my friends. 나의 친구들이야.
→ *A*: ____________________?
B: They are my friends.

6. *Mina* : Please help me. 나 좀 도와줘.
Junwoo: (want, What, you, do)? 넌 무엇을 원해?
→ *Mina* : Please help me.
Junwoo: ____________________?

정답과 해설 p.9

7. *Junwoo*: Sihu leaves Seoul. 시후는 서울을 떠나.

Mina : What? (do, What, I, do) without him ?

뭐라고? 그 없이 나는 무엇을 하라고?

➔ *Junwoo*: Sihu leaves Seoul.

Mina : What? ______________________ without him?

8. *Junwoo*: Just kidding. (*kid: 농담하다 → Just kidding: 농담이야) 농담이야.

Mina : (wrong, is, What) with you? 너에게 무슨 문제가 있어? (도대체 너 왜 그래?)

➔ *Junwoo*: Just kidding.

Mina : ______________________ with you?

9. (is, Who, that girl) over there? 저기 있는 저 여자 애는 누구니?

➔ ______________________ over there?

10. (Who, Mina, teases)? (*tease: 놀리다, 괴롭히다)

누가 미나를 놀리니?

➔ ______________________?

11. (What, Sihu's phone number, is)? 시후의 전화번호는 뭐야?

➔ ______________________?

12. *Emily*: (do, they, What, do) on their birthday?

그들은 생일에 뭘 하니?

Sora : They have a party. 그들은 파티를 열어.

➔ *Emily*: ______________________ on their birthday?

Sora : They have a party.

정답과 해설 p.9

13. (What, going on, is) inside their heads? (*go on: 일어나다, 벌어지다)
그들의 머릿속에서 무엇이 일어나고 있니? (그들이 무슨 생각을 하고 있는 거니?)
➔ ______________________ inside their heads?

14. *Emily*: (What, eat, people, do)? 사람들은 뭘 먹니?
Sora : People eat Tteokguk. 사람들은 떡국을 먹어.
➔ *Emily*: ______________________?
Sora : People eat Tteokguk.

15. *Sihu* : (this place, is, What)? 이 장소는 무엇인가요?
Teacher: This is your new classroom. 여기는 너의 새로운 교실이란다.
➔ *Sihu* : ______________________?
Teacher: This is your new classroom.

16. (your homeroom teacher, is, Who)? 너의 담임선생님은 누구니?
➔ ______________________?

17. (says, Who) that I am a liar? 내가 거짓말쟁이라고 누가 말해?
➔ ______________________ that I am a liar?

18. (you, Who, are)? 넌 누구니?
➔ ______________________?

19. (What, the key, is) to happiness?
행복의 열쇠는 무엇이니?
➔ ______________________ to happiness?

정답과 해설 p.9

Practice 3 알맞은 의문사를 써서 의문문을 완성해 보아요.

우리말 뜻을 참고하여 다음 주어진 의문사와 영어 표현을 사용해 문장을 완성해 보세요.

1. (What, study)

그녀는 무엇을 공부하니?

➔ What does she study ___?

2. (Who, your best friend)

너의 제일 친한 친구는 누구니?

➔ ______ ______?

3. (What, read) 그는 무엇을 읽나요?

➔ ______?

4. (Who, angry) 누가 화났니?

➔ ______?

5. (What, want) 너는 생일 선물로 무엇을 원하니?

➔ ______ for your birthday?

6. (Who, help) 그는 누구를 돕니?

➔ ______?

정답과 해설 p.9

7. (What, bring) 그는 무엇을 가져오니?

➜ ______________________________?

8. (What, do) 너의 친구를 위해 너는 무엇을 해?

➜ ______________________ for your friend?

9. (Who, read a book)

누가 책을 읽니?

➜ ______________________

______________________?

10. (Who, like)

그는 누구를 좋아하니?

➜ ______________________

______________________?

11. (What, your job) 당신의 직업은 무엇인가요?

➜ ______________________________?

12. (What, do) 그녀는 오후에 무엇을 하니?

➜ ______________________ in the afternoon?

13. (What, need) 너는 무엇이 필요하니?

➜ ______________________________?

정답과 해설 p.9

14. (Who, meet) 너는 누구를 만나니?

➔ ______________________________?

15. (What, your plans) 너의 여름방학 계획은 무엇이니?

➔ ____________________ for summer vacation?

16. (Who, visit) 너는 이번 토요일에 누구를 방문하니?

➔ ____________________ this Saturday?

17. (What, your hobby) 너의 취미는 뭐니?

➔ ______________________________?

18. (What, eat)

우리 아침으로 뭘 먹어요?

➔ ____________________

for breakfast?

19. (Who, clean, the bathroom)

누가 화장실을 청소하니? (*bathroom: 화장실, 욕실)

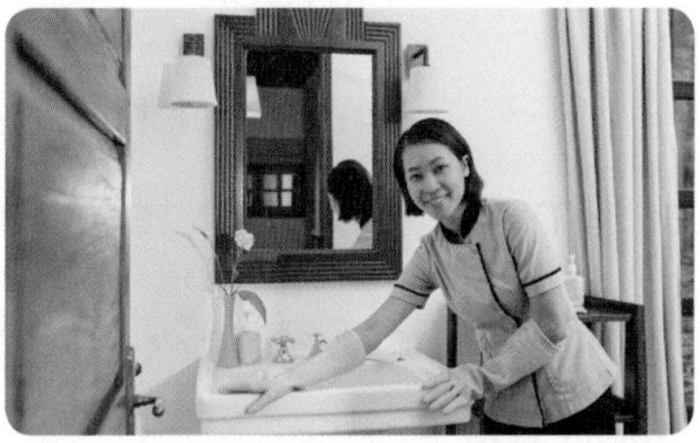

➔ ____________________

____________________?

20. (What, Mina, buy) 미나는 무엇을 사니?

➔ ______________________________?

정답과 해설 p.9

Let's Practice More!

SET 01

학습목표 1 | **be동사가 쓰인 의문사 의문문을 연습해 보아요.** 공부한 날 : 맞은 개수 : /12개

대화의 빈칸에 알맞은 의문사를 넣으세요.

01. *A*: ___What___ is your dream? 너의 꿈은 무엇이니?
B: My dream is to be a doctor. 나의 꿈은 의사가 되는 거야.

02. *A*: __________ is your favorite song? 네가 가장 좋아하는 노래는 무엇이니?
B: My favorite song is "Cheer up". 내가 가장 좋아하는 노래는 'Cheer up'이야.

03. *A*: __________ is angry? 누가 화났니?
B: My father is angry. 나의 아빠가 화나셨어.

04. *A*: __________ is your hobby? 너의 취미는 무엇이니?
B: My hobby is playing the piano. 나의 취미는 피아노를 치는 것이야.

05. *A*: __________ is that girl? 저 여자애는 누구니?
B: She is my younger sister. 그녀는 내 여동생이야.

06. *A*: __________ are you doing tonight? 넌 오늘 밤 무엇을 하니?
B: I'm watching TV tonight. 나는 오늘 밤 TV를 볼거야.

07. *A*: __________ is her name? 그녀의 이름은 무엇이니?
B: Her name is Nayeon. 그녀의 이름은 나연이야.

08. *A*: __________ is he over there? 저기 있는 남자는 누구야?
B: He is my homeroom teacher. 그는 나의 담임 선생님이야.

09. *A*: __________ is wrong? 무슨 일 있어?
B: I failed my English test. 나는 영어시험을 망쳤어.

10. *A*: __________ is this place? 이 장소는 무엇인가요?
B: This is a gym. 이곳은 체육관이야.

11. *A*: __________ is your best friend? 너의 가장 친한 친구는 누구니?
B: My best friend is Mina. 나의 가장 친한 친구는 미나야.

12. *A*: __________ is your job? 너의 직업은 무엇이니?
B: I'm a dentist. 나는 치과의사야.

정답과 해설 p.9

Let's Practice More!

SET 02

학습목표 1 | **be동사가 쓰인 의문사 의문문을 연습해 보아요.** 공부한 날 : 맞은 개수 : /12개

단어들을 순서에 맞게 배열하여 문장을 완성하세요.

01. (is, What, your name)? 너의 이름은 무엇이니?
→ What is your name ?

02. (that little boy, is, Who)? 저 작은 남자아이는 누구니?
→ ____________________?

03. (is, What, that smell)? 저 냄새 뭐야?(무슨 냄새야?)
→ ____________________?

04. (What, that, on your desk, is)? 네 책상 위에 있는 저것은 무엇이니?
→ ____________________?

05. (those people, Who, are)? 저 사람들은 누구야?
→ ____________________?

06. (favorite game, What, your, is)? 네가 가장 좋아하는 게임은 무엇이니?
→ ____________________?

07. (are, doing, you, now, What)? 넌 지금 무엇을 하고 있니?
→ ____________________?

08. (Sihu's, What, phone number, is)? 시후의 전화번호는 무엇이니?
→ ____________________?

09. (your plans, are, What, for vacation)? 너의 방학 계획은 무엇이니?
→ ____________________?

10. (is, your brother, Who)? 누가 너의 오빠이니?
→ ____________________?

11. (your problem, is, What)? 너의 문제는 무엇이니?
→ ____________________?

12. (the key, What, is, to happiness)? 행복의 열쇠는 무엇이니?
→ ____________________?

정답과 해설 p.9

Let's Practice More!

SET 03

학습목표 2 | 일반 동사가 쓰인 의문문을 연습해 보아요. 공부한 날 : 맞은 개수 : /14개

밑줄 친 단어가 맞으면 ○표, 틀리면 고쳐 써 보세요.

01. Who does he meet? 그는 누구를 만나니? → ○

02. Who like Sihu? 누가 시후를 좋아하니? → ________

03. What does I do without him? 그 없이 나는 무엇을 하라고? → ________

04. What does we need? 우리는 뭐가 필요해? → ________

05. Who do she play with? 그녀는 누구와 함께 놀아? → ________

06. Who teases Mina? 누가 미나를 놀리니? → ________

07. What does we eat for breakfast? 우리 아침으로 뭘 먹어요? → ________

08. What do they do on their birthday? 그들은 생일에 뭘 하니? → ________

09. What do she study? 그녀는 무엇을 공부하니? → ________

10. Who does you like? 넌 누구를 좋아해? → ________

11. What does people eat? 사람들은 뭘 먹니? → ________

12. What does she do in winter? 그녀는 겨울에 무엇을 하니? → ________

13. What do you want? 너는 무엇을 원하니? → ________

14. What do Mina buy? 미나는 무엇을 사니? → ________

정답과 해설 p.9

Let's Practice More!

SET 04

학습목표 2 | 일반 동사가 쓰인 의문문을 연습해 보아요. 공부한 날 : 맞은 개수 : /14개

( ) 안에서 알맞은 것을 고르세요.

01. What (do you / you do) want? 너는 무엇을 원하니?

02. What (does he / he does) drink? 그는 무엇을 마시니?

03. Who (you do / do you) visit this Saturday? 너는 이번 토요일에 누구를 방문하니?

04. Who (does he / is he) like? 그는 누구를 좋아하니?

05. What (do you / you do) cook for mom?
너는 엄마를 위해 무엇을 요리하니?

06. What (people do / do people) eat? 사람들은 뭘 먹니?

07. What (does she / she does) do in the afternoon? 그녀는 오후에 무엇을 하니?

08. What (do you / do she) want for your birthday?
너는 생일 선물로 무엇을 원하니?

09. Who (does he / he does) help? 그는 누구를 돕니?

10. What (does they / do they) bring? 그들은 무엇을 가져오니?

11. What (he does / does he) read? 그는 무엇을 읽나요?

12. What (do you do / you do) for your friend? 너의 친구를 위해 너는 무엇을 해?

13. What (do she / do you) need? 너는 무엇이 필요하니?

14. Who (you do / do you) meet? 너는 누구를 만나니?

정답과 해설 p.10

Let's Practice More!

SET 05

학습목표 3 | **what 의문사와 who 의문사를 구별해서 사용할 수 있어요.** 공부한 날 : 맞은 개수 : /14개

다음 문장을 읽고 ( ) 안에서 올바른 단어를 골라 보세요.

01. (What / Who) do you want? 너는 무엇을 원하니?

02. (What / Who) says that I am a liar? 내가 거짓말쟁이라고 누가 말해?

03. (Who / What) reads a book? 누가 책을 읽니?

04. (Who / What) is your job? 당신의 직업은 무엇인가요?

05. (What / Who) is her name? 그녀의 이름은 무엇이니?

06. (What / Who) is angry?
누가 화났니?

07. (Who / What) are your plans for summer vacation? 너의 여름방학 계획은 무엇이니?

08. (Who / What) does she do in the afternoon? 그녀는 오후에 무엇을 하니?

09. (What / Who) do you need? 너는 무엇이 필요하니?

10. (Who / What) do you meet? 너는 누구를 만나니?

11. (What / Who) do you visit this Saturday? 너는 이번 토요일에 누구를 방문하니?

12. (What / Who) do we eat for breakfast? 우리 아침으로 뭘 먹어요?

13. (What / Who) cleans the bathroom?
누가 화장실을 청소하니?

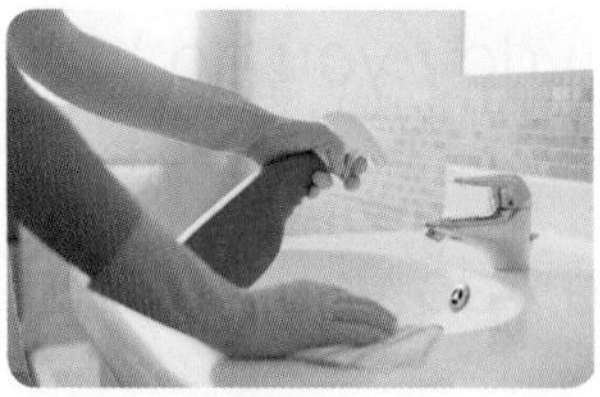

14. (What / Who) does Mina buy? 미나는 무엇을 사니?

정답과 해설 p.10

Let's Practice More!

SET 06

학습목표 3 | **what 의문사와 who 의문사를 구별해서 사용할 수 있어요.** 공부한 날 : 맞은 개수 : /12개

what 또는 who 중에서 적절한 것을 골라 빈칸을 채워보세요.

01. ___What___ can I do for you? 제가 무엇을 해 드릴 수 있을까요?

02. ________ is that girl? 저 여자애는 누구야?

03. ________ is your favorite game?
네가 가장 좋아하는 게임은 뭐야?

04. ________ do you meet? 너는 누구를 만나니?

05. ________ do you like? 넌 누구를 좋아해?

06. ________ do you like? 너는 무엇을 좋아하니?

07. ________ wants to see a movie?
누가 영화를 보고 싶어 하니?

08. ________ is your hobby? 넌 취미가 뭐니?

09. ________ are you doing tonight? 너 오늘 밤에 뭐 할 거야?

10. ________ does she do in winter? 그녀는 겨울에 무엇을 하니?

11. ________ needs my help? 누가 나의 도움이 필요하니?

12. ________ do you want for your birthday?
너는 생일 선물로 무엇을 원하니?

정답과 해설 p.10

Let's Practice More!

SET 07

학습목표 4 | 의문사를 이용한 의문문을 직접 만들어 보아요.   공부한 날 :   맞은 개수 :   /20개

다음 우리말 해석에 맞도록 의문사 what 또는 who를 사용하여 문장을 완성해 보세요.

01. Mom, ___what___ ___do___ we eat for dinner?
엄마, 우리 저녁으로 뭘 먹어요?

02. ________ ________ she study?
그녀는 무엇을 공부하니?

03. ________ ________ that guy over there? 저기 있는 저 남자는 누구니?

04. ________ ________ you need? 너는 무엇이 필요하니?

05. ________ ________ dinner? 누가 저녁을 거르니?

06. ________ ________ that smell? 저 냄새 뭐야? (무슨 냄새야?)

07. ________ ________ that girl? 저 여자애는 누구야?

08. ________ ________ she play with? 그녀는 누구와 함께 놀아?

09. ________ ________ going on inside their heads?
그들의 머릿속에서 무슨 일이 일어나고 있니?

정답과 해설 p.10

10. ___________ ___________ you dislike? 너는 누구를 싫어하니?

11. ___________ ___________ people eat? 사람들은 뭘 먹니?

12. ___________ ___________ your brother? 누가 너의 오빠야?

13. ___________ ___________ he read? 그는 무엇을 읽나요?

14. ___________ ___________ those on your desk?
네 책상 위에 있는 저것들은 뭐야?

15. ___________ ___________ he help? 그는 누구를 돕니?

16. ___________ ___________ she bring? 그녀는 무엇을 가져오니?

17. ___________ ___________ I do without him? 그 없이 나는 무엇을 하라고?

18. ___________ ___________ your plans for summer vacation?
너의 여름방학 계획은 무엇이니?

19. ___________ ___________ wrong with you?
너에게 무슨 문제가 있어? (도대체 너 왜 그래?)

20. ___________ ___________ Mina? 누가 미나를 놀리니?

정답과 해설 p.10

Let's Practice More!

SET 08

학습목표 4 | 의문사를 이용한 의문문을 직접 만들어 보아요. 공부한 날 : 맞은 개수 : /20개

다음 주어진 대답에 어울리는 의문문을 만들어 보세요.

01. I am a dentist.

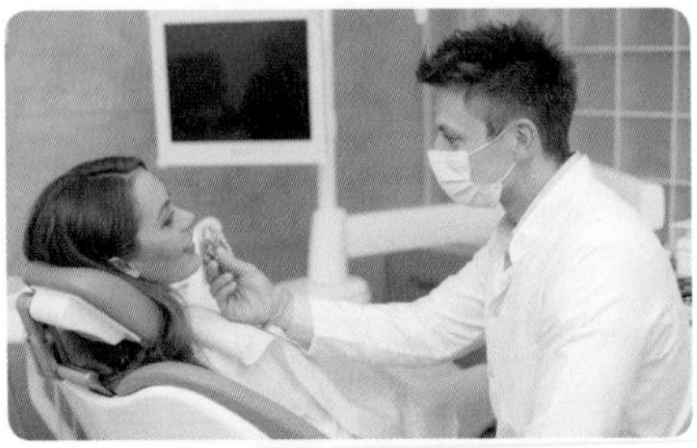

➔ What is your job

_______________?

당신의 직업은 무엇인가요?

02. They have a surprise birthday party.

➔ _______________

_______________?

그들은 그들의 생일에 무엇을 하니?

03. Her name is Mina.

➔ _______________? 그녀의 이름은 무엇이니?

04. My mother wakes me up.

➔ _______________? 누가 너를 깨워줘?

05. He likes Nayeon.

➔ _______________? 그는 누구를 좋아하니?

06. Sihu's phone number is 010-1234-5678.

➔ _______________? 시후의 전화번호는 뭐야?

07. My brother helps you.

➔ _______________? 누가 나를 도와줄 거야?

08. We eat egg toast for breakfast.

➔ _______________?

우리는 아침으로 무엇을 먹어요?

09. My homeroom teacher is Mrs. Kim.

➔ _______________? 너의 담임선생님은 누구니?

정답과 해설 p.10

10. This place is a museum.

➔ ____?

이 장소는 무엇인가요?

11. Mina buys her bag.

➔ ____? 미나가 무엇을 사니?

12. My father cleans the bathroom.

➔ ____? 누가 화장실을 청소하니?

13. The key to happiness is being positive.

➔ ____? 행복의 열쇠는 무엇이니?

14. My best friend is Junwoo.

➔ ____? 너의 제일 친한 친구는 누구니?

15. My math teacher is so angry.

➔ ____? 누가 화났니?

16. I want a bicycle for my birthday present.

➔ ____? 너는 생일 선물로 무엇을 원하니?

17. Those people are Chinese tourists.

➔ ____? 저 사람들은 누구니?

18. My hobby is playing soccer.

➔ ____?

넌 취미가 뭐니?

19. I make cookies for my friend.

➔ ____? 너의 친구를 위해 너는 무엇을 해?

20. My grandmother reads a book.

➔ ____?

누가 책을 읽니?

정답과 해설 p.10

UNIT

when/where 의문문

03 When is your birthday?

❖ POiNT 1 ❖

When은 '언제~'라는 뜻의 의문사예요.

평서문		Your birthday is	next Thursday. 너의 생일은 다음 주 목요일이야.
be동사 의문문		Is your birthday	next Thursday? 너의 생일은 다음 주 목요일이니?
의문사 의문문	When	is your birthday?	너의 생일은 언제니?

When 의문문에 대한 대답은 날짜나 시간으로 해요.

Q: When is your birthday?
너의 생일은 언제니?

A: My birthday is next Monday.
내 생일은 다음 주 월요일이야.

❖ POiNT 2 ❖

Where은 '어디에서~'라는 뜻의 의문사예요.

평서문		He lives	in Seoul.	그는 서울에 살아.
일반동사 의문문		Does he live	in Seoul?	그는 서울에 살아?
의문사 의문문	Where	does he live?		그는 어디에 살아?

Where 의문문에 대한 대답은 장소로 해요.

Q: Where does he live?
그는 어디에 살아?

A: He lives in France.
그는 프랑스에 살아.

Check and Write

다음 주어진 단어들을 순서에 맞게 나열해서 의문문을 완성해 보세요.

1. mother's birthday / is / When ?

When is mother's birthday ?

엄마의 생신은 언제니?

2. you / Where / are ?

______ ?

너 어디에 있어?

3. do / Where / they / play ?

______ ?

그들은 어디에서 놀아?

4. does / When / study / he ?

______ ?

그는 언제 공부해?

5. go / do / we / Where ?

______ ?

우리 어디 가요?

CH 04

정답과 해설 p.10

UNIT

04 Why are you sad?

how/why 의문문

❖ POiNT 1 ❖

How는 '어떻게, 얼마나'라는 뜻의 의문사예요.

평서문		The weather is	sunny.	날씨가 화창해.
be동사 의문문		Is the weather	sunny?	날씨가 화창하니?
의문사 의문문	How	is the weather?		날씨 어때?

How 의문문에 대한 대답은 상태나 방법을 설명하는 말로 해요.

Q: How is the weather?

날씨 어때?

A: It is sunny.

화창해.

❖ POiNT 2 ❖

Why는 '왜~(이유)'라는 뜻의 의문사예요.

평서문		You are	sad.	너는 슬퍼.
be동사 의문문		Are you	sad?	너는 슬퍼?
의문사 의문문	Why	are you	sad?	왜 너는 슬퍼?

Why 의문문에 대한 대답은 주로 because(왜냐하면)를 사용해요.

Q: Why are you sad?

너는 왜 슬퍼?

A: I am sad because my brother is sick.

나는 나의 남동생이 아파서 슬퍼.

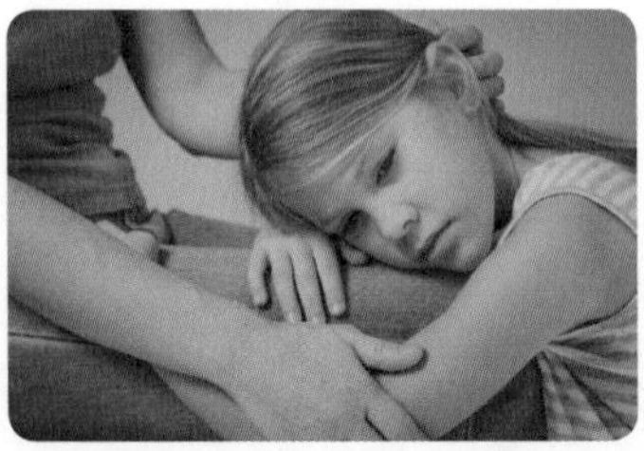

Check and Write

다음 빈칸에 How, Why, Because 중에서 알맞은 것을 넣어 보세요.

1. [How] are you?

너 어떻게 지내?

2. [   ] are you sad?

너는 왜 슬퍼?

3. [   ] I lost my dog.

왜냐하면 난 내 개를 잃어버렸거든.

4. [   ] do you go to school?

너는 학교에 어떻게 가니?

I go to school by bus.

나는 학교에 버스를 타고 가.

5. [   ] is he unhappy?

왜 그가 불행해?

6. [   ] he didn't buy a new bicycle.

왜냐하면 그는 새 자전거를 사지 못했거든.

정답과 해설 p.10

Practice 1 상황에 맞는 의문문과 대답을 익혀 보아요.

다음 문장에 알맞은 단어를 보기 에서 골라 빈칸에 써 보세요.

A Why are you sad?

보기 How Where When Why

1. ___Why___ are you so sad? 너는 왜 그렇게 슬프니?
   I lost my wallet. 지갑을 잃어버렸어.

2. ________ did you lose it? 어떻게 그걸 잃어버렸니?

3. ________ did you lose it? 어디서 그걸 잃어버렸어?

4 ________ did you lose it? 언제 그걸 잃어버렸어?

B I don't need an umbrella!

보기 Because is How Why

1. ________ is the weather today? 오늘 날씨는 어때?

2. It ________ rainy. 비가 와.

3. ________ do you go outside without an umbrella?
   너는 왜 우산 없이 밖에 나가니?

4. ________ I like the rain!
   왜냐하면 난 비를 좋아하니까!

정답과 해설 p.10

C Sihu's day

보기					
Why	When	Where	How	go	do
Because	play	leave	does	takes	arrive

1. __________ do you go to school? 너는 언제 학교에 가?

2. I __________ for school at 8:00. 나는 8시에 학교로 출발해.

3. __________ do you go to school?
너는 학교에 어떻게 가니?

4. I __________ there by bus. 나는 버스를 타고 거기에 가.

5. How long __________ it take to get to school?
학교까지 얼마나 오래 걸려?

6. It __________ about 20 minutes. 약 20분 정도 걸려.

7. When __________ you come back home? 집에 언제 돌아와?

8. I __________ home at 5:00. 난 집에 5시에 도착해.

9. __________ are you so late? 왜 그렇게 늦어?

10. __________ I play soccer after school.
왜냐하면 나는 방과 후에 축구를 하거든.

11. __________ do you play? 어디서 놀아?

12. We __________ in the playground.
우리는 운동장에서 놀아.

정답과 해설 p.10

Practice 2 의문사를 써서 문장을 완성해 보아요.

다음 우리말 뜻과 같도록 주어진 표현을 순서에 맞게 배열하여 문장을 완성하세요.

1. (do, we, eat dinner, When)?

우리 저녁 언제 먹어요?

→ When do we eat dinner ___________?

2. (Where, my dog, is)?

내 개가 어디에 있지?

→ ___________ ___________?

3. (your parents, How, are)? 너희 부모님은 어떻게 지내시니? (너희 부모님은 안녕하시니?)

→ ___________?

4. (from, you, Where, are)? 너는 어디에서 왔니? (너는 어디 출신이니?)

→ ___________?

5. (do, you, Where, want to go)? 너는 어디에 가고 싶어?

→ ___________?

6. (Where, find your dog, do, you)? 너는 어디에서 너의 개를 발견하니?

→ ___________?

정답과 해설 p.10

7. (When, your girlfriend, come, does)? 너의 여자친구는 언제 오니?

➜ ______________________________?

8. (is, my hair, How)? 내 머리 어때요?

➜ ______________________________?

9. *A*: (her, like, Why, you, do)? 넌 그녀가 왜 좋아?

B: Because she is kind! 왜냐하면 그녀는 친절하니까!

➜ *A*: ______________________________?

10. *A*: (Why, you, happy, are)? 너 왜 행복해?

B: Because she smiles at me.

왜냐하면 그녀가 나를 보며 웃으니까.

➜ *A*: ______________________________?

11. (are, How, you)? 너는 어떻게 지내? (안녕?)

➜ ______________________________?

12. (Why, so late, dad, is)? 아빠는 왜 이렇게 늦어요?

➜ ______________________________?

13. *A*: (you, Where, do, live)? 너 어디에 살아?

B: I live next door to you. 나 너희 옆집에 살잖아.

➜ *A*: ______________________________?

정답과 해설 p.10

14. *A*: (When, your birthday, is)? 너의 생일은 언제니?

B: It is April 5th. 4월 5일이야.

➔ *A*: ____?

15. (How, you, know, do)? 네가 어떻게 아니?

➔ ____?

16. (want, you, do, Why) to be a teacher? 너는 왜 선생님이 되길 원해?

➔ ______________________________ to be a teacher?

17. (How, look, I, do)?

나 어때 보여?

➔ ____________________

____________________?

18. (do, buy a cake, you, Why)?

너는 왜 케이크를 사니?

➔ ____________________

____________________?

19. (it, is, How much)? 그것은 얼마니?

➔ ____?

20. (Why, are, busy, you)? 너는 왜 바빠?

➔ ____?

정답과 해설 p.11

Practice 3 상황에 맞는 의문사를 써서 문장을 써 보아요.

우리말 뜻을 참고하여 다음 주어진 표현을 사용해 문장을 완성해 보세요.

1. (Where, go)

너 어디 가?

→ Where do you go ____________?

2. (Why, blame me)

왜 저를 탓하세요?

→ ____________________________?

3. (How, the weather) 날씨 어때?

→ ____________________________?

4. (How, look) 나 어때 보여?

→ ____________________________?

5. (How, feel) 너는 기분이 어떠니?

→ ____________________________?

6. (When, pick you up) 내가 언제 너를 데리러 갈까?

→ ____________________________?

7. (How, know Mina) 네가 미나를 어떻게 알아?

→ ____________________________?

정답과 해설 p.11

8. (Where, study) 넌 어디에서 공부하니?

➔ ____?

9. (How, arrive) *A*: 어떻게 그가 그렇게 일찍 학교에 도착해? *B*: 그는 학교 근처에 살아.

➔ *A*: ______________________ at school so early?

B: He lives near the school.

10. (When, do your homework)

너는 언제 숙제를 해?

➔ ______________________

______________________?

11. (Why, follow me)

너 왜 나 따라와?

➔ ______________________

______________________?

12. (How, know each other) 너희들은 서로 어떻게 알아?

➔ ____?

13. (Where, we, meet) 우리 어디서 만나?

➔ ____?

14. (When, we, meet) 우리 언제 만나지?

➔ ____?

정답과 해설 p.11

15. (When, wake up)

너는 언제 일어나니?

➔ ______________________

______________________?

16. (Where, the dog, sleep)

그 개는 어디서 자니?

➔ ______________________

______________________?

17. (Where, the bookstore) *A*: 서점은 어디 있니? *B*: 빵집 옆에 있어.

➔ *A*: ______________________________________?

B: It is next to the bakery.

18. (When, the store, open) 그 상점은 언제 열어?

➔ ______________________________________?

19. (Why, nice to me) *A*: 너 나한테 왜 잘해줘? *B*: 왜냐하면 나는 너를 좋아하니까.

➔ *A*: ______________________________?

B: Because I like you.

20. (Why, great) *A*: 왜 그가 훌륭해? *B*: 왜냐하면 그는 불쌍한 사람들을 돕거든.

➔ *A*: ______________________________________?

B: Because he helps poor people.

정답과 해설 p.11

Let's Practice More!

SET 01

학습목표 1 | **When, Where, Why, How 의문사를 구별해 보아요.** 공부한 날 : 맞은 개수 : /12개

다음 우리말 해석에 맞도록 ( ) 안에서 올바른 단어를 골라 보세요.

01. (Why / Where) are you so sad? 너는 왜 그렇게 슬프니?

02. (How / When) did you lose it? 너는 어떻게 그걸 잃어버렸니?

03. (When / Where) do you go to school? 너는 언제 학교에 가?

04. (Why / How) do you go to school? 너는 학교에 어떻게 가니?

05. (How / When) long does it take to get to school? 학교까지 얼마나 오래 걸려?

06. (When / Why) are you so late? 너는 왜 그렇게 늦어?

07. (Where / How) do you play? 너는 어디서 놀아?

08. (Where / When) do we eat dinner? 우리 저녁 언제 먹어요?

09. (Where / How) is my dog? 내 개가 어디에 있지?

10. (How / Where) do you want to go? 너는 어디에 가고 싶어?

11. (How / Why) is my hair? 내 머리 어때요?

12. (When / Why) do you like her? 넌 그녀가 왜 좋아?

정답과 해설 p.11

Let's Practice More!

SET 02

학습목표 1 | **When, Where, Why, How 의문사를 구별해 보아요.** 공부한 날 : 맞은 개수 : /14개

다음 우리말 해석을 보고 밑줄 친 단어가 맞으면 ○표, 틀리면 고쳐 써 보세요.

01. How are you? 너는 어떻게 지내니? → ○

02. How is dad so late? 아빠는 왜 이렇게 늦어요? → ______

03. Where is your birthday? → ______
너의 생일은 언제니?

04. How do you know? 네가 어떻게 아니? → ______

05. Why do you buy a cake? 너는 왜 케이크를 사니? → ______

06. Where do you go? 너 어디 가? → ______

07. How do I pick you up? 내가 언제 너를 데리러 갈까? → ______

08. Where do you study? → ______
넌 어디에서 공부하니?

09. How do you do your homework? 너는 언제 숙제를 해? → ______

10. Where do you follow me? 너 왜 나 따라와? → ______

11. Where do we meet? 우리 어디서 만나? → ______

12. How do we meet? 우리 언제 만나지? → ______

13. How does he arrive at school so early? → ______
어떻게 그가 그렇게 일찍 학교에 도착해?

14. When are you nice to me? 너 나한테 왜 잘해줘? → ______

정답과 해설 p.11

Let's Practice More!

SET 03

학습목표 2 | 의문문의 배열을 주의 깊게 관찰해 보아요.　　공부한 날 :　　맞은 개수 :　　/14개

다음 문장을 읽고 밑줄 친 부분의 단어가 올바른 자리에 있으면 ○표, 아니면 ×표를 하세요.

01. Where did you lose it? 너는 어디서 그걸 잃어버렸어? → ○

02. How is the weather today? 오늘 날씨는 어때? → ______

03. Do how you go to school? 너는 학교에 어떻게 가니? → ______

04. How long does it take to get to school? 학교까지 얼마나 오래 걸려? → ______

05. Do when you come back home? 집에 언제 돌아와? → ______

06. Are where you from? 너는 어디 출신이니? → ______

07. Do where you want to go? 너는 어디에 가고 싶어? → ______

08. Why do you like her? 넌 그녀가 왜 좋아? → ______

09. Are how you? 너는 어떻게 지내니? → ______

10. Is why dad so late? 아빠는 왜 이렇게 늦어요? → ______

11. Why do you buy a cake? 너는 왜 케이크를 사니? → ______

12. How much is it? 그것은 얼마니? → ______

13. Why are you busy? 너는 왜 바빠? → ______

14. Do why you blame me? 왜 저를 탓하세요? → ______

정답과 해설 p.11

Let's Practice More!

SET 04

학습목표 2 | 의문문의 배열을 주의 깊게 관찰해 보아요.　　공부한 날 :　　맞은 개수 :　　/12개

( ) 안에서 올바른 것을 골라 보세요.

01. (Where do / Do where) you live? 너 어디에 살아?

02. (Do how / How do) I look? 나 어때 보여?

03. (Is how / How is) the weather? 날씨 어때?

04. (Do how / How do) you know Mina? 네가 미나를 어떻게 알아?

05. (Where do / Do where) you study? 넌 어디에서 공부하니?

06. (When do / Do when) we meet? 우리 언제 만나지?

07. (Does where / Where does) the dog sleep? 그 개는 어디서 자니?

08. (Does when / When does) the store open?
그 상점은 언제 열어?

09. (Is why / Why is) he great? 왜 그가 훌륭해?

10. (When did / Did when) you lose it? 언제 그걸 잃어버렸어?

11. (Why do / Do why) you go outside without an umbrella? 너는 왜 우산 없이 밖에 나가니?

12. (Do when / When do) you come back home? 너는 집에 언제 돌아와?

정답과 해설 p.11

Let's Practice More!

SET 05

학습목표 2 | 의문문의 배열을 주의 깊게 관찰해 보아요. 공부한 날 : 맞은 개수 : /14개

다음 빈칸에 들어갈 말로 알맞은 것을 채워보세요.

01. Where ___do___ you play? 너는 어디서 놀아?

02. When ________ we eat dinner? 우리 저녁 언제 먹어요?

03. Where ________ my dog? 내 개가 어디에 있지?

04. How ________ your parents? 너희 부모님은 어떻게 지내시니?(너희 부모님은 안녕하시니?)

05. Where ________ you from? 너는 어디에서 왔니?(너는 어디 출신이니?)

06. When ________ your girlfriend come? 너의 여자친구는 언제 오니?

07. How ________ my hair? 내 머리 어때요?

08. Why ________ you happy? 너 왜 행복해?

09. Where ________ you live? 너 어디에 살아?

10. When ________ your birthday? 너의 생일은 언제니?

11. How ________ you know? 네가 어떻게 아니?

12. Why ________ you want to be a teacher? 너는 왜 선생님이 되길 원해?

13. How ________ you feel? 너는 기분이 어떠니?

14. Where ________ the dog sleep? 그 개는 어디서 자니?

정답과 해설 p.11

Let's Practice More!

SET 06

학습목표 3 | 의문문에 답해 보아요. 　　공부한 날 : 　　맞은 개수 : 　/14개

( ) 안의 표현을 사용하여 다음 의문문에 대한 대답을 완성해 보세요.

01. How is the weather today? (rainy) 오늘 날씨는 어때?

➜ It ___is___ ___rainy___.

비가 와.

02. How do you go to school? (go)

너는 학교에 어떻게 가니?

➜ ________ ________ there by bus.

나는 그곳에 버스를 타고 가.

03. Why do you go outside without an umbrella? (rain) 너는 왜 우산 없이 밖에 나가니?

➜ Because ________ ________ the ________!

왜냐하면 난 비를 좋아하니까!

04. When do you go to school? (school) 너는 언제 학교에 가?

➜ I leave for ________ ________ 8 a.m.

나는 아침 8시에 학교로 출발해.

05. How long does it take to get to school? (minutes) 학교까지 얼마나 오래 걸려?

➜ It ________ about 20 ________. 약 20분 정도 걸려.

06. When do you come back home? (arrive) 집에 언제 돌아와?

➜ I ________ ________ at 5:00. 난 집에 5시에 도착해.

정답과 해설 p.11

07. Why are you so late? (soccer) 넌 왜 그렇게 늦어?

➔ Because I __________ ________________ after school.

왜냐하면 나는 방과 후에 축구를 하거든.

08. Where do you play? (playground) 너희들은 어디서 놀아?

➔ We __________ in the ________________. 우리는 운동장에서 놀아.

09. When does your girlfriend come? (arrive) 너의 여자친구는 언제 오니?

➔ She will ________________ soon. 그녀는 곧 도착할 거야.

10. Why are you happy? (present) 너 왜 행복해?

➔ __________ my parents gave me a __________.

왜냐하면 나의 부모님이 나에게 선물을 주셨거든.

11. How do I look? (happy) 나 어때 보여?

➔ You __________ so __________. 정말 행복해 보여.

12. Where do you go? (my friend) 너 어디 가?

➔ I go to __________ __________ __________. 나는 친구를 만나러 가.

13. Why are you busy? (homework)

너는 왜 바빠?

➔ __________ I have a lot of ________________.

왜냐하면 나는 숙제가 많거든.

14. How do you know each other? (classmates) 너희들은 서로 어떻게 알아?

➔ We __________ ________________.

우리는 같은 반이야.

정답과 해설 p.11

Let's Practice More!

SET 07

학습목표 4 | 의문사를 이용한 의문문을 직접 만들어 보아요. 공부한 날 : 맞은 개수 : /20개

다음 우리말 해석에 맞도록 빈칸을 채워 문장을 완성해 보세요.

01. ___Why___ ___are___ you so sad? 너는 왜 그렇게 슬프니?

02. ________ ________ you know him? 너는 어떻게 그를 알아?

03. ________ ________ is it? 그것은 얼마니?

04. ________ ________ he live? 그는 어디에 사니?

05. ________ ________ you want to go? 너는 어디에 가고 싶니?

06. ________ ________ you blame me? 왜 저를 탓하세요?

07. ________ ________ the weather? 날씨 어때?

08. ________ ________ you feel? 너는 기분이 어떠니?

09. ________ ________ I pick you up? 내가 언제 너를 데리러 갈까?

10. ________ ________ you know Mina? 네가 미나를 어떻게 알아?

11. ________ ________ you know each other? 너희들은 서로 어떻게 알아?

12. ________ ________ we meet? 우리 어디서 만나?

13. ________ ________ you wake up? 너는 언제 일어나니?

14. ________ ________ the bookstore? 서점은 어디 있니?

15. ________ ________ he arrive at school so early? 어떻게 그가 그렇게 일찍 학교에 도착해?

16. ________ ________ you nice to me? 너 나한테 왜 잘해줘?

17. ________ ________ he great? 왜 그가 훌륭해?

18. ________ ________ you go to school? 너는 언제 학교에 가?

19. ________ ________ my dog? 내 개가 어디에 있지?

20. ________ ________ the store open? 그 상점은 언제 열어?

정답과 해설 p.11

Let's Practice More!

SET 08

학습목표 4 | **의문사를 이용한 의문문을 직접 만들어 보아요.** 공부한 날 : 맞은 개수 : /20개

다음 대답에 어울리는 의문문을 완성해 보세요.

01. *A*: ______How is______ the weather? 날씨는 어때?

B: It is rainy. 비가 와.

02. *A*: ____________________ so late? 왜 그렇게 늦어?

B: Because I play soccer after school.

왜냐하면 나는 방과 후에 축구를 하거든.

03. *A*: ____________________ go outside without an umbrella?

너는 왜 우산 없이 밖에 나가니?

B: Because I like the rain! 왜냐하면 난 비를 좋아하니까!

04. A: ____________________ go to school? 너는 언제 학교에 가?

B: I leave for school at 8:00. 나는 8시에 학교로 출발해.

05. *A*: ____________________ go to school? 너는 학교에 어떻게 가니?

B: I go there by bus. 나는 버스를 타고 거기에 가.

06. *A*: ____________________? 너희들은 어디서 놀아?

B: We play in the playground. 우리는 운동장에서 놀아.

07. *A*: ____________________ does it take to get to school? 학교까지 얼마나 오래 걸려?

B: It takes about 20 minutes. 약 20분 정도 걸려.

08. *A*: ____________________ come back home? 집에 언제 돌아와?

B: I arrive home at 5:00. 난 집에 5시에 도착해.

09. *A*: ____________________ eat dinner? 우리 저녁 언제 먹어요?

B: We eat dinner at 8:00. 우리는 8시에 저녁을 먹어.

정답과 해설 p.11

10. A: ______________________ did you find your dog? 너는 어디에서 너의 개를 발견했니?

B: I found my dog under the desk. 나는 내 개를 책상 밑에서 발견했어.

11. A: ______________________ want to be a teacher?

너는 왜 선생님이 되길 원해?

B: Because I like teaching. 왜냐하면 난 가르치는 것을 좋아하니까.

12. A: ______________________ do your homework? 너는 언제 숙제를 해?

B: I do my homework after dinner. 나는 저녁을 먹고 나서 숙제를 해.

13. A: ______________________ follow me? 너 왜 나 따라와?

B: Because you dropped your smartphone. 왜냐하면 넌 너의 스마트폰을 떨어뜨렸으니까.

14. A: ______________________ wake up? 너는 언제 일어나니?

B: I wake up at 7:00. 나는 7시에 일어나.

15. A: ______________________ the bookstore? 서점은 어디 있니?

B: The bookstore is next to the school. 서점은 학교 옆에 있어.

16. A: ______________________ the store open? 그 상점은 언제 열어?

B: The store opens early in the morning. 그 상점은 아침 일찍 열어.

17. A: ______________________ so sad? 너는 왜 그렇게 슬프니?

B: Because I lost my wallet. 왜냐하면 난 내 지갑을 잃어버렸거든.

18. A: ______________________? 너는 어디에서 왔니?(너는 어디 출신이니?)

B: I'm from Canada. 나는 캐나다에서 왔어.

19. A: ______________________? 넌 그녀가 왜 좋아?

B: Because she is kind. 왜냐하면 그녀는 친절하니까.

20. A: ______________________________ a cake?

너는 왜 케이크를 사니?

B: Because today is my mom's birthday.

왜냐하면 오늘은 나의 엄마의 생일이거든.

정답과 해설 p.11

실전테스트

CHAPTER 03~04

공부한 날 :

복습한 날 :

부모님 확인 :

CHAPTER 03 일반동사의 부정문과 의문문 CHAPTER 04 의문사 의문문

● 정답과 해설은 별책 12쪽에서 확인하세요!!

01

다음 대화의 빈칸에 공통으로 들어갈 알맞은 단어를 고르세요.

A: Who is he?
B: He is my cousin.
A: ________ he play soccer?
B: Yes, he ________.

① Do[do] ② Does[does]
③ What[what] ④ Is[is]

[02~03] 다음 빈칸에 알맞은 말을 쓰세요.

02

A: What (1) ____________ this?

B: This (2) ____________ my notebook.

03

A: (1) ____________ she have many books?

B: Yes, she (2) ____________.

04

다음 문장을 부정문으로 만들 때 not이 들어갈 자리를 고르세요.

He ① does ② sing ③ a ④ song.

____

05

다음 그림을 보고, 주어진 철자로 시작하는 단어를 넣어 대화를 완성하세요.

A: H_______ d_______ you go to school?

B: I go to school by bus.

06

다음 그림을 참고하여 빈칸에 알맞은 말을 쓰세요.

A: ____________ ____________ he wake up?
(그는 언제 일어납니까?)

B: He wakes up at seven.
(그는 7시에 일어납니다.)

07

다음 그림을 보고, 빈칸에 들어갈 알맞은 단어를 고르세요.

A: ________ do you like?
B: I like him.

① When ② Who
③ What ④ How

08

다음 중 어색한 문장을 고르세요.

① I'm not busy.
② She doesn't go camping.
③ They're not writers.
④ It do not jump high.

[09~10] 다음 문장을 바르게 고쳐 다시 쓰세요. (단, 인칭대명사는 바꾸지 마세요.)

09

Do he wear a coat?

10

What does you see?

11

다음 그림을 보고, [보기]에서 알맞은 말을 골라 대화를 완성하세요.

[보기] When, What, Do, Does

A: __________ do you exercise?
B: In the morning.
A: __________ you go jogging?
B: Yes, I do.

[12~14] 다음 대화의 빈칸에 들어갈 알맞은 단어를 쓰세요.

12

A: When (1) __________ your birthday?
B: My birthday (2) __________ August 5th.

13

A: (1) __________ he play the piano?
B: Yes, he (2) __________.

14

A: (1) __________ you like vegetables?
B: Yes, I (2) __________.

15
다음 빈칸에 들어갈 알맞은 단어를 고르세요.

A: ________ is he?
B: He is my cousin.

① Who ② When
③ What ④ Where

[16-17] 다음 문장을 부정문으로 바꿔 쓰세요.

16
I need a rest.

⇨ ______________________________

17
She wants to go there.

⇨ ______________________________

[18~19] 다음 단어들을 순서에 맞게 배열하여 의문문을 완성하세요.

18
(he / Does / like / running)?

⇨ ______________________________

19
(you / want / Do / puppy / a)?

⇨ ______________________________

[20~21] 다음 빈칸에 들어갈 알맞은 단어를 고르세요.

20
__________ does she live?
그녀는 어디에 사니?

① What ② Who
③ Where ④ When

21
__________ is the problem?
무엇이 문제니?

① Why ② What
③ How ④ When

[22~23] 다음 대화를 읽고, 물음에 답하세요.

A: _______ ⓐ _______
B: I like soccer.
A: Would you like to go to a soccer game tomorrow?
B: That sounds great!

22
대화의 빈칸 ⓐ에 들어갈 질문으로 알맞은 것을 고르세요.

① What do you want to do?
② What do you like?
③ Who is your favorite player?
④ How is your vacation?

23
대화에서 두 사람이 내일 할 일을 우리말로 적으세요.

⇨ ______________________________

[24-25] 다음 단어를 배열하여 문장을 쓰세요.

24

(does, walk, She, to, school, not).

⇨ ______________________________

25

(he, Does, bread, bake)?

⇨ ______________________________

26

대화를 읽고, 빈칸에 알맞은 말끼리 순서대로 짝지어진 것을 고르세요.

A: Hello. ________ you from Japan?
B: No, I'm from Korea. I'm Insu.
A: ________ do you spell your name?
B: I-N-S-U.

① Are, Where ② Where, What
③ How, What ④ Are, How

27

다음 중 어색한 문장을 고르세요.

① Do you have a pet?
② Do they play table tennis?
③ Does Kevin's parents get up early?
④ Do Insu and Sumin study hard?

[28~29] 다음 문장을 의문문으로 바꿔 쓰세요.

28

Mary likes cats.

⇨ ______________________________

(Mary는 고양이를 좋아해?)

29

You study English.

⇨ ______________________________

(너는 영어를 공부하니?)

30

다음 빈칸에 들어갈 말로 알맞지 않은 것을 고르세요.

They ________.

① does not live in Busan
② wash the dishes
③ are not my friends
④ don't watch TV

실전테스트

Cultural Tips
재미로 익히는 문화상식

각 나라의 특이한 행운의 미신

중국
새해 첫째 날과 둘째 날에는 행운이 함께 날아갈 수 있다고 생각해서 절대 청소하지 않는대요!

스페인
1월1일 12시가 되면 서로에게 행운을 빌면서 종이 한 번 칠 때마다 한 알씩 12개의 청포도를 먹는대요!

러시아
집, 자동차, 사람에게 새똥이 떨어지면 돈이 들어온다고 믿어요!

프랑스
왼발로 강아지 똥을 밟으면 행운이 오고, 오른발로 강아지 똥을 밟으면 불행이 온다는 미신이 있대요!

Cultural Tips
재미로 익히는 문화상식

여러 나라의 독특한 교통수단

이탈리아의 곤돌라(Gondola)
이탈리아 베네치아 시내에 있는 운하를 운항하는 배예요.
11세기부터 주요 교통수단으로 사용되었지만, 요즘은 수가 적어졌다고 해요.

유럽의 트램(노면전차)(Tram, streetcar)
주로 도로에 만들어진 선로를 따라 전기로 움직이는 전동차를 뜻해요.
독일, 러시아, 우크라이나를 비롯한 나라에서 주로 도시 안이나 근교에서 이동수단으로 이용된다고 해요.

인도네시아와 자전거 택시 베짝(Becak)
자전거 뒤에 인력거가 붙어 있고 운전수가 승객이 원하는 곳까지 운전해줘요.
베짝은 서민들에게는 중요한 교통수단 중 하나라고 해요.

초등영문법3800제 LEVEL 2

워크북

WORKBOOK

1. **단어 쓰기 연습** mp3 음성 파일을 듣고 들려주는 단어를 세 번씩 써 보아요.
2. **Dictation Test** mp3 음성 파일을 듣고 빈칸을 채워 보세요.
3. **단어테스트** 단어 쓰기 연습을 하며 암기한 단어들을 제대로 외웠는지 확인해 보아요.
4. **워크북 정답** Dictation Test와 단어테스트의 정답

초등영문법3800제 MP3 파일 이용 방법

1. 홈페이지에서 다운로드

① 마더텅 홈페이지(www.toptutor.co.kr) 접속 → 상단 메뉴 중 [초등 · 유아]의 [교재 소개] 선택 → 교재 목록에서 해당 교재명 찾아 선택 → 학습자료의 [mp3] 선택 후 다운로드

② 마더텅 홈페이지(www.toptutor.co.kr) 접속 → 상단 메뉴 중 [초등 · 유아] 의 [교재자료실] 선택 → 자료실 상단의 [교재를 선택하세요.] 에서 해당 교재명 선택 → 자료 목록에서 mp3 게시물 선택 후 다운로드

2. 모바일 스트리밍 / 다운로드

① 스마트폰으로 교재 뒷면의 QR코드 스캔 → MP3 스트리밍 or 다운로드

② 주소창에 m.toptutor.co.kr 또는 포털에서 '마더텅' 검색 → [MP3 자료실] 선택 → 상단 메뉴 중 [초등 · 유아] 선택 → 해당 교재명 찾아 선택 후 MP3 스트리밍 or 다운로드

단어 쓰기 연습 1

초3800_2_d1

들려주는 단어를 잘 듣고, 세 번씩 써 보세요.

MP3 2권 단어 01

01 **walk** ⓓ 걷다	walk		
02 **read** ⓓ 읽다	read		
03 **swim** ⓓ 수영하다	swim		
04 **study** ⓓ 공부하다	study		
05 **hate** ⓓ 싫어하다	hate		
06 **want** ⓓ 원하다	want		
07 **wish** ⓓ 바라다	wish		
08 **know** ⓓ 알다	know		
09 **think** ⓓ 생각하다	think		
10 **doll** ⓜ 인형	doll		
11 **family** ⓜ 가족	family		
12 **weekend** ⓜ 주말	weekend		
13 **American** ⓜ 미국인	American		

들려주는 단어를 잘 듣고, 세 번씩 써 보세요.

MP3 2권 단어 01

14 **rise** 동 떠오르다	rise		
15 **east** 명 동쪽	east		
16 **wake** 동 (잠에서) 깨다	wake		
17 **cook** 동 요리하다	cook		
18 **live** 동 살다	live		
19 **breakfast** 명 아침식사	breakfast		
20 **tooth** 명 이, 치아	tooth		
21 **brush** 동 닦다	brush		
22 **quickly** 부 빨리	quickly		
23 **nag** 동 잔소리하다	nag		
24 **listen** 동 듣다	listen		
25 **sleep** 동 자다	sleep		
26 **afternoon** 명 오후	afternoon		

단어 쓰기 연습 2

초3800_2_d2

들려주는 단어를 잘 듣고, 세 번씩 써 보세요.

MP3 2권 단어 02

27 **tomorrow** 명 내일	tomorrow		
28 **vacation** 명 방학	vacation		
29 **hard** 부 열심히	hard		
30 **keep** 동 유지하다	keep		
31 **homework** 명 숙제	homework		
32 **test** 명 시험	test		
33 **flu** 명 독감	flu		
34 **dislike** 동 싫어하다	dislike		
35 **shot** 명 주사	shot		
36 **fever** 명 열	fever		
37 **fall** 동 넘어지다	fall		
38 **again** 부 다시	again		
39 **warm** 형 따뜻한	warm		

들려주는 단어를 잘 듣고, 세 번씩 써 보세요.

MP3 2권 단어 02

40 **hug** ⓜ 포옹	hug		
41 **book** ⓜ 책	book		
42 **habit** ⓜ 버릇	habit		
43 **secret** ⓜ 비밀	secret		
44 **special** ⓗ 특별한	special		
45 **talent** ⓜ 재능	talent		
46 **destroy** ⓓ 파괴하다	destroy		
47 **enemy** ⓜ 적	enemy		
48 **curious** ⓗ 호기심 많은	curious		
49 **need** ⓓ 필요하다	need		
50 **break** ⓜ 휴식	break		
51 **until** ⓙ ~까지	until		
52 **hurry** ⓜ 급함	hurry		

초3800_2_d3

단어 쓰기 연습 3

들려주는 단어를 잘 듣고, 세 번씩 써 보세요.

MP3 2권 단어 **03**

01 **work** ⓓ 일하다	work		
02 **say** ⓓ 말하다	say		
03 **prepare** ⓓ 준비하다	prepare		
04 **eat** ⓓ 먹다	eat		
05 **run** ⓓ 달리다	run		
06 **fast** ⓑ 빨리, 빠르게	fast		
07 **drive** ⓓ 운전하다	drive		
08 **office** ⓜ 사무실	office		
09 **always** ⓑ 항상	always		
10 **pass** ⓓ 통과하다	pass		
11 **exam** ⓜ 시험	exam		
12 **finish** ⓓ 끝내다	finish		
13 **touch** ⓓ 만지다	touch		

들려주는 단어를 잘 듣고, 세 번씩 써 보세요.

MP3 2권 단어 03

14 **relax** ⓓ 휴식을 취하다	relax		
15 **cry** ⓓ 울다	cry		
16 **make** ⓓ 만들다	make		
17 **open** ⓓ 열다	open		
18 **meat** ⓜ 고기	meat		
19 **wash** ⓓ 씻다	wash		
20 **cut** ⓓ 자르다	cut		
21 **onion** ⓜ 양파	onion		
22 **clean** ⓓ 청소하다	clean		
23 **table** ⓜ 식탁	table		
24 **spoon** ⓜ 숟가락	spoon		
25 **chopsticks** ⓜ 젓가락	chopsticks		
26 **science** ⓜ 과학	science		

단어 쓰기 연습 4

초3800_2_d4

들려주는 단어를 잘 듣고, 세 번씩 써 보세요.

MP3 2권 단어 04

27 **play** ⓓ 연주하다	play		
28 **picture** ⓜ 사진	picture		
29 **answer** ⓜ 해답	answer		
30 **solve** ⓓ 해결하다	solve		
31 **problem** ⓜ 문제	problem		
32 **happy** ⓗ 행복한	happy		
33 **happen** ⓓ 발생하다	happen		
34 **odd** ⓗ 이상한	odd		
35 **sound** ⓓ ~처럼 들리다	sound		
36 **wolf** ⓜ 늑대	wolf		
37 **cold** ⓜ 감기	cold		
38 **save** ⓓ 구하다	save		
39 **bird** ⓜ 새	bird		

들려주는 단어를 잘 듣고, 세 번씩 써 보세요.

MP3 2권 단어 **04**

40	**lesson**	명 교훈	lesson
41	**life**	명 생명	life
42	**mailman**	명 우체부	mailman
43	**deliver**	동 배달하다	deliver
44	**letter**	명 편지	letter
45	**wear**	동 입다	wear
46	**uniform**	명 제복	uniform
47	**send**	동 보내다	send
48	**leaf**	명 (나뭇) 잎	leaf
49	**dentist**	명 치과의사	dentist
50	**voice**	명 목소리	voice
51	**drink**	동 마시다	drink
52	**bake**	동 굽다	bake

단어 쓰기 연습 5

초3800_2_d5

들려주는 단어를 잘 듣고, 세 번씩 써 보세요.

MP3 2권 단어 05

01 **sleepy** 형 졸음이 오는	sleepy		
02 **grown-up** 명 어른	grown-up		
03 **late** 형 늦은	late		
04 **fool** 명 바보	fool		
05 **classroom** 명 교실	classroom		
06 **bored** 형 지루해하는	bored		
07 **baby** 명 아기	baby		
08 **awake** 형 깨어 있는	awake		
09 **hungry** 형 배고픈	hungry		
10 **angry** 형 화난	angry		
11 **friend** 명 친구	friend		
12 **cat** 명 고양이	cat		
13 **dancer** 명 무용수	dancer		

들려주는 단어를 잘 듣고, 세 번씩 써 보세요.

MP3 2권 단어 05

14 **singer** 명 가수	singer		
15 **sister** 명 여자형제	sister		
16 **kind** 형 친절한	kind		
17 **brother** 명 남자형제	brother		
18 **student** 명 학생	student		
19 **funny** 형 웃긴	funny		
20 **soccer** 명 축구	soccer		
21 **player** 명 (운동) 선수	player		
22 **fast** 형 빠른	fast		
23 **little** 형 (크기가) 작은	little		
24 **tall** 형 (키가) 큰	tall		
25 **mean** 형 심술궂은	mean		
26 **lazy** 형 게으른	lazy		

단어 쓰기 연습 6

초3800_2_d6

들려주는 단어를 잘 듣고, 세 번씩 써 보세요.

MP3 2권 단어 06

27 **teacher** ⓜ 교사, 선생	teacher		
28 **strict** ⓗ 엄격한	strict		
29 **parents** ⓜ 부모	parents		
30 **grandparents** ⓜ 조부모	grandparents		
31 **city** ⓜ 도시	city		
32 **smart** ⓗ 똑똑한	smart		
33 **happy** ⓗ 행복한	happy		
34 **child** ⓜ 아이, 어린이	child		
35 **tired** ⓗ 피곤한	tired		
36 **inside** ⓙ ~의 안에	inside		
37 **house** ⓜ 집	house		
38 **happiness** ⓜ 행복	happiness		
39 **far** ⓑ 멀리	far		

들려주는 단어를 잘 듣고, 세 번씩 써 보세요.

MP3 2권 단어 06

단어			
40 **young** ⓗ 어린	young		
41 **real** ⓗ 실제의	real		
42 **weak** ⓗ 약한	weak		
43 **sure** ⓗ 확실한	sure		
44 **afraid** ⓗ 두려워하는	afraid		
45 **easy** ⓗ 쉬운	easy		
46 **thirsty** ⓗ 목마른	thirsty		
47 **best** ⓗ 최고의	best		
48 **same** ⓗ 같은	same		
49 **clean** ⓗ 깨끗한	clean		
50 **important** ⓗ 중요한	important		
51 **problem** ⓜ 문제	problem		
52 **webtoon** ⓜ 웹툰	webtoon		

단어 쓰기 연습 7

초3800_2_d7

들려주는 단어를 잘 듣고, 세 번씩 써 보세요.

MP3 2권 단어 07

01 **onion** ㊐ 양파	onion		
02 **trust** ㊐ 믿다	trust		
03 **know** ㊐ 알다	know		
04 **matter** ㊐ 중요하다	matter		
05 **hurt** ㊐ 다치게 하다	hurt		
06 **smile** ㊐ 웃다	smile		
07 **lie** ㊐ 거짓말하다	lie		
08 **bag** ㊐ 가방	bag		
09 **tooth** ㊐ 이, 치아	tooth		
10 **homework** ㊐ 숙제	homework		
11 **break** ㊐ 휴식	break		
12 **need** ㊐ 필요하다	need		
13 **party** ㊐ 파티	party		

들려주는 단어를 잘 듣고, 세 번씩 써 보세요.

MP3 2권 단어 07

14 **science** ⓜ 과학	science		
15 **test** ⓜ 시험	test		
16 **share** ⓢ 공유하다	share		
17 **food** ⓜ 음식	food		
18 **vegetable** ⓜ 야채	vegetable		
19 **basketball** ⓜ 농구	basketball		
20 **badminton** ⓜ 배드민턴	badminton		
21 **walk** ⓢ 걷다	walk		
22 **come** ⓢ 오다	come		
23 **lunch** ⓜ 점심(식사)	lunch		
24 **baseball** ⓜ 야구	baseball		
25 **sleep** ⓢ 잠자다	sleep		
26 **socks** ⓜ 양말	socks		

단어 쓰기 연습 8

초3800_2_d8

들려주는 단어를 잘 듣고, 세 번씩 써 보세요.

MP3 2권 단어 **08**

27 **wear** ⓓ 입다	wear		
28 **summer** ⓜ 여름	summer		
29 **kind** ⓗ 친절한	kind		
30 **movie** ⓜ 영화	movie		
31 **remember** ⓓ 기억하다	remember		
32 **birthday** ⓜ 생일	birthday		
33 **picture** ⓜ 사진	picture		
34 **duck** ⓜ 오리	duck		
35 **club activity** ⓜ 동아리 활동	club activity		
36 **jump** ⓓ 뛰다	jump		
37 **time** ⓜ 시간	time		
38 **blue** ⓗ 파란	blue		
39 **color** ⓜ 색	color		

들려주는 단어를 잘 듣고, 세 번씩 써 보세요.

MP3 2권 단어 08

40 **fight** ⓓ 싸우다	fight		
41 **library** ⓜ 도서관	library		
42 **breakfast** ⓜ 아침(식사)	breakfast		
43 **health** ⓜ 건강	health		
44 **noise** ⓜ 소음	noise		
45 **swim** ⓓ 수영하다	swim		
46 **turtle** ⓜ 거북	turtle		
47 **bean** ⓜ 콩	bean		
48 **watch** ⓓ 보다	watch		
49 **math** ⓜ 수학	math		
50 **church** ⓜ 교회	church		
51 **muffler** ⓜ 목도리	muffler		
52 **snack** ⓜ 간식	snack		

단어 쓰기 연습 9

초3800_2_d9

들려주는 단어를 잘 듣고, 세 번씩 써 보세요.

MP3 2권 단어 **09**

01	**toy** ⓜ 장난감	toy			
02	**want** ⓢ 원하다	want			
03	**leave** ⓢ 떠나다	leave			
04	**favorite** ⓗ 가장 좋아하는	favorite			
05	**meet** ⓢ 만나다	meet			
06	**friend** ⓜ 친구	friend			
07	**blueberry** ⓜ 블루베리	blueberry			
08	**cake** ⓜ 케이크	cake			
09	**present** ⓜ 선물	present			
10	**name** ⓜ 이름	name			
11	**cook** ⓢ 요리하다	cook			
12	**study** ⓢ 공부하다	study			
13	**birthday** ⓜ 생일	birthday			

들려주는 단어를 잘 듣고, 세 번씩 써 보세요.

MP3 2권 단어 09

14 **movie** ⑱ 영화	movie		
15 **hobby** ⑱ 취미	hobby		
16 **tonight** ⑮ 오늘 밤에	tonight		
17 **winter** ⑱ 겨울	winter		
18 **dinner** ⑱ 저녁(식사)	dinner		
19 **skip** ⑧ 건너뛰다	skip		
20 **smell** ⑱ 냄새	smell		
21 **help** ⑧ 돕다	help		
22 **play** ⑧ 놀다	play		
23 **people** ⑱ 사람들	people		
24 **woman** ⑱ 여자	woman		
25 **desk** ⑱ 책상	desk		
26 **letter** ⑱ 편지	letter		

단어 쓰기 연습 10

초3800_2_d10

들려주는 단어를 잘 듣고, 세 번씩 써 보세요.

MP3 2권 단어 **10**

27	**without**	전 ~없이	without
28	**wrong**	형 틀린, 잘못된	wrong
29	**tease**	동 놀리다	tease
30	**phone number**	명 전화번호	phone number
31	**inside**	전 ~의 안에	inside
32	**head**	명 머리	head
33	**place**	명 장소	place
34	**new**	형 새로운	new
35	**say**	동 말하다	say
36	**liar**	명 거짓말쟁이	liar
37	**key**	명 열쇠	key
38	**happiness**	명 행복	happiness
39	**read**	동 읽다	read

들려주는 단어를 잘 듣고, 세 번씩 써 보세요.

MP3 2권 단어 10

40 **angry** ⓗ 화난	angry		
41 **bring** ⓓ 가져오다	bring		
42 **buy** ⓓ 사다	buy		
43 **job** ⓜ 직업	job		
44 **afternoon** ⓜ 오후	afternoon		
45 **plan** ⓜ 계획	plan		
46 **summer** ⓜ 여름	summer		
47 **vacation** ⓜ 방학	vacation		
48 **visit** ⓓ 방문하다	visit		
49 **Saturday** ⓜ 토요일	Saturday		
50 **clean** ⓓ 청소하다	clean		
51 **bathroom** ⓜ 욕실	bathroom		
52 **go** ⓓ 가다	go		

단어 쓰기 연습 11

초3800_2_d11

들려주는 단어를 잘 듣고, 세 번씩 써 보세요.

MP3 2권 단어 11

01 **live** ⓢ 살다	live		
02 **France** ⓜ 프랑스	France		
03 **when** ⓑ 언제	when		
04 **where** ⓑ 어디에	where		
05 **weather** ⓜ 날씨	weather		
06 **sunny** ⓗ 화창한	sunny		
07 **sad** ⓗ 슬픈	sad		
08 **sick** ⓗ 아픈	sick		
09 **lose** ⓢ 잃어버리다	lose		
10 **school** ⓜ 학교	school		
11 **unhappy** ⓗ 불행한	unhappy		
12 **buy** ⓢ 사다	buy		
13 **bicycle** ⓜ 자전거	bicycle		

들려주는 단어를 잘 듣고, 세 번씩 써 보세요.

MP3 2권 단어 11

14 **how** ㊕ 어떻게	how		
15 **why** ㊕ 왜	why		
16 **because** ㊎ 왜냐하면	because		
17 **today** ㊔ 오늘	today		
18 **rainy** ㊖ 비가 오는	rainy		
19 **outside** ㊕ 바깥에, 밖에	outside		
20 **without** ㊍ ~없이	without		
21 **umbrella** ㊔ 우산	umbrella		
22 **rain** ㊔ 비	rain		
23 **playground** ㊔ 놀이터, 운동장	playground		
24 **from** ㊍ ~출신의	from		
25 **find** ㊐ 찾다	find		
26 **girlfriend** ㊔ 여자친구	girlfriend		

단어 쓰기 연습 12

초3800_2_d12

들려주는 단어를 잘 듣고, 세 번씩 써 보세요.

MP3 2권 단어 12

27 **come** ㉭ 오다	come		
28 **hair** ㉮ 머리카락	hair		
29 **smile** ㉭ 웃다	smile		
30 **late** ㉯ 늦은	late		
31 **door** ㉮ 문	door		
32 **next** ㉯ 옆의	next		
33 **April** ㉮ 4월	April		
34 **look** ㉭ ~하게 보이다	look		
35 **busy** ㉯ 바쁜	busy		
36 **blame** ㉭ 비난하다	blame		
37 **feel** ㉭ 느끼다	feel		
38 **know** ㉭ 알다	know		
39 **arrive** ㉭ 도착하다	arrive		

들려주는 단어를 잘 듣고, 세 번씩 써 보세요.

MP3 2권 단어 12

40 **early** ⓗ 이른	early		
41 **near** ⓙ ~에서 가까이	near		
42 **homework** ⓜ 숙제	homework		
43 **follow** ⓓ 따라가다	follow		
44 **store** ⓜ 가게	store		
45 **bookstore** ⓜ 서점	bookstore		
46 **bakery** ⓜ 빵집	bakery		
47 **open** ⓓ 문을 열다	open		
48 **nice** ⓗ 좋은, 멋진	nice		
49 **great** ⓗ 위대한	great		
50 **help** ⓓ 돕다	help		
51 **poor** ⓗ 불쌍한	poor		
52 **people** ⓜ 사람들	people		

초3800_2_d1

Dictation Test 1

MP3 2권 받아쓰기 01

Name : Date : Score : /10

[01~10] 들려주는 문장을 잘 듣고 빈칸에 알맞은 단어를 채워 보세요.

01. I ________________ Mondays.
    나는 월요일이 싫다.

02. I ________________ ________________ ________________ quickly.
    나는 빠르게 양치를 한다.

03. I ________________ to school at eight.
    나는 8시에 걸어서 학교에 간다.

04. Mina ________________ weekends.
    미나는 주말을 좋아한다.

05. We ________________ a vacation!
    우린 방학을 원해!

06. I ________________ hard.
    나는 공부를 열심히 해.

07. I ________________ ________________ with my friends.
    나는 친구들과 축구를 한다.

08. I ________________ shots!
    나는 주사가 싫어!

09. We ________________ many books.
    우리는 책을 많이 읽어.

10. They ________________ ice cream.
    그들은 아이스크림을 먹는다.

정답 p.204

초3800_2_d2

Dictation Test 2

MP3 2권 받아쓰기 02

Name : Date : Score : /10

[01~10] 들려주는 문장을 잘 듣고 빈칸에 알맞은 단어를 채워 보세요.

01. We ________ ________ ________ first.
우리는 먼저 우리의 숙제를 한다.

02. You ________ well.
너는 수영을 잘한다.

03. I ________ no special talents.
나는 특별한 재능들을 가지고 있지 않다.

04. Mom ________ ________ ________.
엄마가 그녀를 깨운다.

05. She ________ a sweet dream every day.
그녀는 매일 좋은 꿈을 꾼다.

06. Mom, I ________ ________ ________.
엄마, 나 열나요.

07. I ________ an English test next Monday.
난 다음 주 월요일에 영어시험을 쳐.

08. I ________ ________ late.
나는 늦게 일어나.

09. Ms. Lee ________ English.
이 선생님은 영어를 가르치신다.

10. I ________ your help.
나는 너의 도움이 필요해.

정답 p.204

초3800_2_d3

Dictation Test 3

MP3 2권 받아쓰기 03

Name : Date : Score : /10

[01~10] 들려주는 문장을 잘 듣고 빈칸에 알맞은 단어를 채워 보세요.

01. My mom ________________ watching TV.
나의 엄마는 TV를 보는 것을 좋아하셔.

02. Mina ________________ a doll.
미나는 인형을 원해.

03. My little brother ________________ a lot.
내 남동생은 많이 먹어.

04. Nayeon ________________ fast.
나연이는 빨리 달려.

05. Dad ________________ ________________ his office.
아빠는 차를 타고 사무실로 가셔.

06. She ________________ hard.
그녀는 열심히 공부해.

07. Mina ________________ ________________ ________________ by bus.
미나는 버스를 타고 학교로 가.

08. Hayul ________________ every morning.
하율이는 매일 아침 울어.

09. She ________________ English.
그녀는 영어를 가르치셔.

10. He ________________ many books.
그는 많은 책을 가지고 있어.

정답 p.204

초3800_2_d4

Dictation Test 4

MP3 2권 받아쓰기 04

Name : Date : Score : /10

[01~10] 들려주는 문장을 잘 듣고 빈칸에 알맞은 단어를 채워 보세요.

01. He ________________ the refrigerator.
그는 냉장고를 열어.

02. My mother ________________ the vegetables.
나의 엄마는 야채를 씻어요.

03. My mom ________________ ________________ the school.
나의 엄마는 학교에서 일하셔.

04. She ________________ ________________ ________________ the students.
그녀는 학생들에게 인사를 해요.

05. Bakers ________________ bread.
제빵사들은 빵을 구워요.

06. Mina ________________ a letter.
미나는 편지를 보내요.

07. Sihu ________________ board games.
시후는 보드게임을 한다.

08. My dog ________________ me.
나의 개는 나에게 뽀뽀를 해.

09. My sister ________________ the violin.
나의 언니는 바이올린을 연주해.

10. She ________________ taking pictures.
그녀는 사진 찍는 걸 아주 좋아해.

정답 p.204

초3800_2_d5

Dictation Test 5

MP3 2권 받아쓰기 05

Name : Date : Score : /10

[01~10] 들려주는 문장을 잘 듣고 빈칸에 알맞은 단어를 채워 보세요.

01. She ________________ a grown-up.
그녀는 어른이 아니야.

02. I ________________ ________________ a fool!
난 바보가 아니야!

03. They ________________ in the classroom.
그들은 교실에 있지 않아.

04. He ________________ sleepy.
그는 졸리지 않아.

05. We ________________ bored.
우리들은 지루하지 않아.

06. The baby ________________ awake.
그 아기는 깨어있지 않아.

07. ________________ ________________ your friend?
그녀는 네 친구니?

08. ________________ ________________ late?
너 늦었니?

09. ________________ ________________ at home?
그는 집에 있어?

10. ________________ ________________ a cat?
그것은 고양이야?

정답 p.204

초3800_2_d6

Dictation Test 6

MP3 2권 받아쓰기 **06**

Name : Date : Score : /10

[01~10] 들려주는 문장을 잘 듣고 빈칸에 알맞은 단어를 채워 보세요.

01. He ________ ________ funny.
그는 재밌지 않아.

02. ________ ________ tired?
너는 피곤하니?

03. They ________ ________ young.
그들은 어리지 않아.

04. ________ ________ your best friend?
그는 너의 가장 친한 친구니?

05. I ________ ________ a good rapper.
나는 랩을 못 해.

06. Are you ________ ________ school?
너는 학교에 늦니?

07. ________ ________ afraid of birds?
당신은 새를 무서워하나요?

08. ________ ________ ________ easy.
그것은 쉽지 않아.

09. Our classroom ________ ________ ________.
우리 교실은 깨끗하지 않다.

10. ________ ________ a soccer player?
그는 축구선수야?

정답 p.204

초3800_2_d7

Dictation Test 7

MP3 2권 받아쓰기 07

Name : Date : Score : /10

[01~10] 들려주는 문장을 잘 듣고 빈칸에 알맞은 단어를 채워 보세요.

01. I ________________ hurt you.

나는 너를 해치지 않아.

02. She ________________ smile.

그녀는 웃지 않아.

03. They ________________ lie.

그들은 거짓말하지 않아.

04. ________________ ________________ talk.

너는 말하지 않아.

05. ________________ ________________ have homework?

그녀는 숙제가 있니?

06. ________________ ________________ need a break?

너는 휴식이 필요하니?

07. ________________ ________________ have a brother?

그는 형제가 있니?

08. ________________ ________________ have a party?

그들은 파티를 하니?

09. Do ________________ ________________ vegetables?

너는 야채를 먹니?

10. ________________ your father ________________ badminton?

너의 아버지는 배드민턴을 치시니?

정답 p.204

초3800_2_d8

Dictation Test 8

MP3 2권 받아쓰기 08

Name : Date : Score : /10

[01~10] 들려주는 문장을 잘 듣고 빈칸에 알맞은 단어를 채워 보세요.

01. Eric ________ ________ TV shows.
    Eric은 TV 쇼를 보지 않는다.

02. I ________ ________ time to sleep.
    나는 잘 시간이 없다.

03. ________ ducks ________ fast?
    오리가 빨리 걷니?

04. ________ ________ eat fish?
    너희는 생선을 먹니?

05. They ________ ________ to the mall.
    그들은 쇼핑몰에 가지 않는다.

06. I ________ ________ Karen's birthday.
    나는 Karen의 생일이 기억나지 않는다.

07. ________ ________ play games a lot?
    내가 게임을 많이 하니?

08. I ________ ________ breakfast.
    나는 아침밥을 먹지 않는다.

09. I ________ ________ a watch.
    나는 손목시계를 차지 않는다.

10. ________ you ________ the color blue?
    너는 파란색을 좋아하니?

정답 p.204

초3800_2_d9

Dictation Test 9

MP3 2권 받아쓰기 09

Name : Date : Score : /10

[01~10] 들려주는 문장을 잘 듣고 빈칸에 알맞은 단어를 채워 보세요.

01. ________________ does he want?
그는 무엇을 원하니?

02. ________________ do you leave?
너는 언제 떠나니?

03. ________________ ________________ your favorite food?
네가 가장 좋아하는 음식은 무엇이니?

04. Who do you ________________ ?
너는 누구를 만나니?

05. ________________ do you go?
너는 어디에 가니?

06. ________________ is that girl?
저 여자애는 누구야?

07. What ________________ your name?
너의 이름이 무엇이니?

08. Who is your ________________ ?
누가 너의 언니야?

09. ________________ do you like?
너는 무엇을 좋아하니?

10. Who ________________ cooking?
누가 요리하는 것을 좋아하니?

정답 p.204

초3800_2_d10

Dictation Test 10

MP3 2권 받아쓰기 10

Name : Date : Score : /10

[01~10] 들려주는 문장을 잘 듣고 빈칸에 알맞은 단어를 채워 보세요.

01. What does she ________________ ?
그녀는 무엇을 공부하니?

02. Who ________________ she play with?
그녀는 누구와 함께 놀아?

03. ________________ do you need?
너는 무엇이 필요하니?

04. ________________ is your best friend?
너의 제일 친한 친구는 누구니?

05. What ________________ Mina buy?
미나는 무엇을 사니?

06. What do people ________________ ?
사람들은 뭘 먹니?

07. ________________ is angry?
누가 화났니?

08. ________________ is that on your desk?
네 책상 위에 있는 저건 뭐야?

09. Who ________________ me?
누가 나를 도와줄 거야?

10. ________________ is your hobby?
넌 취미가 뭐니?

정답 p.204

초3800_2_d11

Dictation Test 11

MP3 2권 받아쓰기 11

Name : Date : Score : /10

[01~10] 들려주는 문장을 잘 듣고 빈칸에 알맞은 단어를 채워 보세요.

01. ________________ is mother's birthday?

엄마의 생일이 언제야?

02. ________________ are you?

너 어디에 있어?

03. Where ________________ they ________________ ?

그들은 어디에서 놀아?

04. When ________________ ________________ study?

그는 언제 공부해?

05. ________________ do we go?

우리 어디 가요?

06. ________________ ________________ ________________ ?

너 어떻게 지내?

07. Why ________________ you so ________________ ?

너는 왜 그렇게 슬프니?

08. ________________ do you live?

너 어디에 살아?

09. How ________________ you ________________ to school?

너는 학교에 어떻게 가니?

10. ________________ is he unhappy?

왜 그가 불행해?

정답 p.204

초3800_2_d12

Dictation Test 12

MP3 2권 받아쓰기 12

Name : Date : Score : /10

[01~10] 들려주는 문장을 잘 듣고 빈칸에 알맞은 단어를 채워 보세요.

01. ________ is the weather today?
오늘 날씨는 어때?

02. Why ________ you ________ her?
넌 그녀가 왜 좋아?

03. ________ is my hair?
내 머리 어때요?

04. ________ is the bookstore?
서점은 어디 있니?

05. When ________ the store ________ ?
그 상점은 언제 열어?

06. ________ do you wake up?
너는 언제 일어나니?

07. ________ ________ you follow me?
너 왜 나 따라와?

08. Where ________ ________ meet?
우리 어디서 만나?

09. Why ________ ________ busy?
너는 왜 바빠?

10. ________ ________ is it?
그것은 얼마니?

정답 p.204

단어테스트 1

다음 한글 뜻을 보고 영어 표현을 적으세요. Name : Date : Score : /26

01		동 걷다	14		동 떠오르다
02		동 읽다	15		명 동쪽
03		동 수영하다	16		동 (잠에서) 깨다
04		동 공부하다	17		동 요리하다
05		동 싫어하다	18		동 살다
06		동 원하다	19		명 아침식사
07		동 바라다	20		명 이, 치아
08		동 알다	21		동 닦다
09		동 생각하다	22		부 빨리
10		명 인형	23		동 잔소리하다
11		명 가족	24		동 듣다
12		명 주말	25		동 자다
13		명 미국인	26		명 오후

정답 p.204

단어테스트 2

다음 한글 뜻을 보고 영어 표현을 적으세요. Name : Date : Score : /26

01		명 내일	
02		명 방학	
03		부 열심히	
04		동 유지하다	
05		명 숙제	
06		명 시험	
07		명 독감	
08		동 싫어하다	
09		명 주사	
10		명 열	
11		동 넘어지다	
12		부 다시	
13		형 따뜻한	
14		명 포옹	
15		명 책	
16		명 버릇	
17		명 비밀	
18		형 특별한	
19		명 재능	
20		동 파괴하다	
21		명 적	
22		형 호기심이 많은	
23		동 필요하다	
24		명 휴식	
25		전 ~까지	
26		명 급함	

정답 p.204

단어테스트 3

다음 한글 뜻을 보고 영어 표현을 적으세요. Name : Date : Score : /26

01		동 일하다	14		동 휴식을 취하다
02		동 말하다	15		동 울다
03		동 준비하다	16		동 만들다
04		동 먹다	17		동 열다
05		동 달리다	18		명 고기
06		부 빨리, 빠르게	19		동 씻다
07		동 운전하다	20		동 자르다
08		명 사무실	21		명 양파
09		부 항상	22		동 청소하다
10		동 통과하다	23		명 식탁
11		명 시험	24		명 숟가락
12		동 끝내다	25		명 젓가락
13		동 만지다	26		명 과학

정답 p.204

단어테스트 4

다음 한글 뜻을 보고 영어 표현을 적으세요. Name : Date : Score : /26

01		동 연주하다	14		명 교훈
02		명 사진	15		명 생명
03		명 해답	16		명 우체부
04		동 해결하다	17		동 배달하다
05		명 문제	18		명 편지
06		형 행복한	19		동 입다
07		동 발생하다	20		명 제복
08		형 이상한	21		동 보내다
09		동 ~처럼 들리다	22		명 (나뭇) 잎
10		명 늑대	23		명 치과의사
11		명 감기	24		명 목소리
12		동 구하다	25		동 마시다
13		명 새	26		동 굽다

정답 p.204

단어테스트 5

다음 한글 뜻을 보고 영어 표현을 적으세요. Name : Date : Score : /26

01		형 졸음이 오는	14		명 가수
02		명 어른	15		명 여자형제
03		형 늦은	16		형 친절한
04		명 바보	17		명 남자형제
05		명 교실	18		명 학생
06		형 지루해하는	19		형 웃긴
07		명 아기	20		명 축구
08		형 깨어 있는	21		명 (운동) 선수
09		형 배고픈	22		형 빠른
10		형 화난	23		형 (크기가) 작은
11		명 친구	24		형 (키가) 큰
12		명 고양이	25		형 심술궂은
13		명 무용수	26		형 게으른

정답 p.204

단어테스트 6

다음 한글 뜻을 보고 영어 표현을 적으세요. Name : Date : Score : /26

01		명 교사, 선생	14		형 어린
02		형 엄격한	15		형 실제의
03		명 부모	16		형 약한
04		명 조부모	17		형 확실한
05		명 도시	18		형 두려워하는
06		형 똑똑한	19		형 쉬운
07		형 행복한	20		형 목마른
08		명 아이, 어린이	21		형 최고의
09		형 피곤한	22		형 같은
10		전 ~의 안에	23		형 깨끗한
11		명 집	24		형 중요한
12		명 행복	25		명 문제
13		부 멀리	26		명 웹툰

정답 p.205

단어테스트 7

다음 한글 뜻을 보고 영어 표현을 적으세요. Name : Date : Score : /26

01		명 양파	14		명 과학
02		동 믿다	15		명 시험
03		동 알다	16		동 공유하다
04		동 중요하다	17		명 음식
05		동 다치게 하다	18		명 야채
06		동 웃다	19		명 농구
07		동 거짓말하다	20		명 배드민턴
08		명 가방	21		동 걷다
09		명 이, 치아	22		동 오다
10		명 숙제	23		명 점심(식사)
11		명 휴식	24		명 야구
12		동 필요하다	25		동 잠자다
13		명 파티	26		명 양말

정답 p.205

단어테스트 8

다음 한글 뜻을 보고 영어 표현을 적으세요. Name : Date : Score : /26

01		동 입다	14		동 싸우다
02		명 여름	15		명 도서관
03		형 친절한	16		명 아침(식사)
04		명 영화	17		명 건강
05		동 기억하다	18		명 소음
06		명 생일	19		동 수영하다
07		명 사진	20		명 거북
08		명 오리	21		명 콩
09		명 동아리 활동	22		동 보다
10		동 뛰다	23		명 수학
11		명 시간	24		명 교회
12		형 파란	25		명 목도리
13		명 색	26		명 간식

정답 p.205

단어테스트 9

다음 한글 뜻을 보고 영어 표현을 적으세요. Name : Date : Score : /26

01 ______ 명 장난감

02 ______ 동 원하다

03 ______ 동 떠나다

04 ______ 형 가장 좋아하는

05 ______ 동 만나다

06 ______ 명 친구

07 ______ 명 블루베리

08 ______ 명 케이크

09 ______ 명 선물

10 ______ 명 이름

11 ______ 동 요리하다

12 ______ 동 공부하다

13 ______ 명 생일

14 ______ 명 영화

15 ______ 명 취미

16 ______ 부 오늘 밤에

17 ______ 명 겨울

18 ______ 명 저녁(식사)

19 ______ 동 건너뛰다

20 ______ 명 냄새

21 ______ 동 돕다

22 ______ 동 놀다

23 ______ 명 사람들

24 ______ 명 여자

25 ______ 명 책상

26 ______ 명 편지

정답 p.205

단어테스트 10

다음 한글 뜻을 보고 영어 표현을 적으세요. Name : Date : Score : /26

01		전 ~없이	14		형 화난
02		형 틀린, 잘못된	15		동 가져오다
03		동 놀리다	16		동 사다
04		명 전화번호	17		명 직업
05		전 ~의 안에	18		명 오후
06		명 머리	19		명 계획
07		명 장소	20		명 여름
08		형 새로운	21		명 방학
09		동 말하다	22		동 방문하다
10		명 거짓말쟁이	23		명 토요일
11		명 열쇠	24		동 청소하다
12		명 행복	25		명 욕실
13		동 읽다	26		동 가다

정답 p.205

단어테스트 11

다음 한글 뜻을 보고 영어 표현을 적으세요. Name : Date : Score : /26

01		동 살다	14		부 어떻게
02		명 프랑스	15		부 왜
03		부 언제	16		접 왜냐하면
04		부 어디에	17		명 오늘
05		명 날씨	18		형 비가 오는
06		형 화창한	19		부 바깥에, 밖에
07		형 슬픈	20		전 ~없이
08		형 아픈	21		명 우산
09		동 잃어버리다	22		명 비
10		명 학교	23		명 놀이터, 운동장
11		형 불행한	24		전 ~출신의
12		동 사다	25		동 찾다
13		명 자전거	26		명 여자친구

정답 p.205

단어테스트 12

다음 한글 뜻을 보고 영어 표현을 적으세요. Name : Date : Score : /26

01		동 오다	14		형 이른
02		명 머리카락	15		전 ~에서 가까이
03		동 웃다	16		명 숙제
04		형 늦은	17		동 따라가다
05		명 문	18		명 가게
06		형 옆의	19		명 서점
07		명 4월	20		명 빵집
08		동 ~하게 보이다	21		동 문을 열다
09		형 바쁜	22		형 좋은, 멋진
10		동 비난하다	23		형 위대한
11		동 느끼다	24		동 돕다
12		동 알다	25		형 불쌍한
13		동 도착하다	26		명 사람들

정답 p.205

워크북 정답

Dictation Test 1

01. hate
02. brush, my, teeth
03. walk
04. likes
05. want
06. study
07. play, soccer
08. hate
09. read
10. eat

Dictation Test 2

01. do, our, homework
02. swim
03. have
04. wakes, her, up
05. has
06. have, a, fever
07. have
08. get, up
09. teaches
10. need

Dictation Test 3

01. likes
02. wants
03. eats
04. runs
05. drives, to
06. studies
07. goes, to, school
08. cries
09. teaches
10. has

Dictation Test 4

01. opens
02. washes
03. works, at
04. says, hello, to
05. bake
06. sends
07. plays
08. kisses
09. plays
10. loves

Dictation Test 5

01. isn't
02. am, not
03. aren't
04. isn't
05. aren't
06. isn't
07. Is, she
08. Are, you
09. Is, he
10. Is, it

Dictation Test 6

01. is, not
02. Are, you
03. are, not
04. Is, he
05. am, not
06. late, for
07. Are, you
08. It, is, not
09. is, not, clean
10. Is, he

Dictation Test 7

01. don't
02. doesn't
03. don't
04. You, don't
05. Does, she
06. Do, you
07. Does, he
08. Do, they
09. you, eat
10. Does, play

Dictation Test 8

01. doesn't, watch
02. don't, have
03. Do, walk
04. Do, you
05. don't, go
06. don't, remember
07. Do, I
08. don't, eat
09. don't, wear
10. Do, like

Dictation Test 9

01. What
02. When
03. What, is
04. meet
05. Where
06. Who
07. is
08. sister
09. What
10. likes

Dictation Test 10

01. study
02. does
03. What
04. Who
05. does
06. eat
07. Who
08. What
09. helps
10. What

Dictation Test 11

01. When
02. Where
03. do, play
04. does, he
05. Where
06. How, are, you
07. are, sad
08. Where
09. do, go
10. Why

Dictation Test 12

01. How
02. do, like
03. How
04. Where
05. does, open
06. When
07. Why, do
08. do, we
09. are, you
10. How, much

단어테스트 1

01. walk
02. read
03. swim
04. study
05. hate
06. want
07. wish
08. know
09. think
10. doll
11. family
12. weekend
13. American
14. rise
15. east
16. wake
17. cook
18. live
19. breakfast
20. tooth
21. brush
22. quickly
23. nag
24. listen
25. sleep
26. afternoon

단어테스트 2

01. tomorrow
02. vacation
03. hard
04. keep
05. homework
06. test
07. flu
08. dislike
09. shot
10. fever
11. fall
12. again
13. warm
14. hug
15. book
16. habit
17. secret
18. special
19. talent
20. destroy
21. enemy
22. curious
23. need
24. break
25. until
26. hurry

단어테스트 3

01. work
02. say
03. prepare
04. eat
05. run
06. fast
07. drive
08. office
09. always
10. pass
11. exam
12. finish
13. touch
14. relax
15. cry
16. make
17. open
18. meat
19. wash
20. cut
21. onion
22. clean
23. table
24. spoon
25. chopsticks
26. science

단어테스트 4

01. play
02. picture
03. answer
04. solve
05. problem
06. happy
07. happen
08. odd
09. sound
10. wolf
11. cold
12. save
13. bird
14. lesson
15. life
16. mailman
17. deliver
18. letter
19. wear
20. uniform
21. send
22. leaf
23. dentist
24. voice
25. drink
26. bake

단어테스트 5

01. sleepy
02. grown-up
03. late

04. fool
05. classroom
06. bored
07. baby
08. awake
09. hungry
10. angry
11. friend
12. cat
13. dancer
14. singer
15. sister
16. kind
17. brother
18. student
19. funny
20. soccer
21. player
22. fast
23. little
24. tall
25. mean
26. lazy

단어테스트 6

01. teacher
02. strict
03. parents
04. grandparents
05. city
06. smart
07. happy
08. child
09. tired
10. inside
11. house
12. happiness
13. far
14. young
15. real
16. weak
17. sure
18. afraid
19. easy
20. thirsty
21. best
22. same
23. clean
24. important
25. problem
26. webtoon

단어테스트 7

01. onion
02. trust
03. know
04. matter
05. hurt
06. smile
07. lie
08. bag
09. tooth
10. homework
11. break
12. need
13. party
14. science
15. test
16. share
17. food
18. vegetable
19. basketball
20. badminton
21. walk
22. come
23. lunch
24. baseball
25. sleep
26. socks

단어테스트 8

01. wear
02. summer
03. kind
04. movie
05. remember
06. birthday
07. picture
08. duck
09. club activity
10. jump
11. time
12. blue
13. color
14. fight
15. library
16. breakfast
17. health
18. noise
19. swim
20. turtle
21. bean
22. watch
23. math
24. church
25. muffler
26. snack

단어테스트 9

01. toy
02. want
03. leave
04. favorite
05. meet
06. friend
07. blueberry
08. cake
09. present
10. name
11. cook
12. study
13. birthday
14. movie
15. hobby
16. tonight
17. winter
18. dinner
19. skip
20. smell
21. help
22. play
23. people
24. woman
25. desk
26. letter

단어테스트 10

01. without
02. wrong
03. tease
04. phone number
05. inside
06. head
07. place
08. new
09. say
10. liar
11. key
12. happiness
13. read
14. angry
15. bring
16. buy
17. job
18. afternoon
19. plan
20. summer
21. vacation
22. visit
23. Saturday
24. clean
25. bathroom
26. go

단어테스트 11

01. live
02. France
03. when
04. where
05. weather
06. sunny
07. sad
08. sick
09. lose
10. school
11. unhappy
12. buy
13. bicycle
14. how
15. why
16. because
17. today
18. rainy
19. outside
20. without
21. umbrella
22. rain
23. playground
24. from
25. find
26. girlfriend

단어테스트 12

01. come
02. hair
03. smile
04. late
05. door
06. next
07. April
08. look
09. busy
10. blame
11. feel
12. know
13. arrive
14. early
15. near
16. homework
17. follow
18. store
19. bookstore
20. bakery
21. open
22. nice
23. great
24. help
25. poor
26. people

Grammar Review

초등영문법 3800제 2권에서 배운 문법 내용을 한 번 더 정리해 보아요!

보기에서 알맞은 말을 골라 빈칸에 넣으세요.

※ 정답은 뒷면(p.208)에 있습니다.

be동사의 부정문

보 기: not / aren't / 없어요 / 뒤 / isn't

1 be동사의 부정문은 be동사의 __________에 __________을 넣어서 만들 수 있어요.

2 be동사의 부정형은 줄여서 쓸 수 있어요. 아래의 빈칸을 채워보세요.

주어	be동사	부정형	줄임말
I	am	am not	X
He / She / It	is	is not	's not / __________
We / You / They	are	are not	're not / __________

3 I am not의 am not은 줄일 수 __________.

일반동사의 부정문

보 기: do not / does not / 앞 / don't / doesn't / 동사원형 (중복 사용 가능)

1 일반동사의 부정문을 만들 때 주어가 I, You, 복수형이면 일반동사의 __________에 __________을 넣어서 만들어요.

2 그러나 주어가 3인칭 단수일 때는 일반동사의 __________에 __________을 넣어서 부정문을 만들어요.

3 부정문에서 do not이나 does not 뒤의 일반동사는 __________이 와요.

4 do not은 __________로 줄여 쓸 수 있어요.

5 does not은 __________로 줄여 쓸 수 있어요.

✎ 보기에서 알맞은 말을 골라 빈칸에 넣으세요.

의문사로 의문문 만들기

보 기: 문장 맨 앞 / what / where / when / how / why / who

1 6개의 의문사에는 ______________(누가), ______________(언제), ______________(어디서), ______________(무엇을), ______________(어떻게), ______________(왜)가 있어요.

2 의문사를 이용해 의문문을 만들 때에는 be동사 의문문 또는 일반동사 의문문의 ______________에 의문사를 붙어주면 돼요.

그래머 리뷰

일반동사의 3인칭 단수형

보 기: has / –s / –es / i
(중복 사용 가능)

1 일반동사의 3인칭 단수형을 만들 때 대부분은 동사 뒤에 ______________를 붙여요.

2 동사가 「자음+y」로 끝나면 y를 ______________로 고치고 ______________를 붙여요.
(cries, studies, tries)

3 –s, –sh, –ch, –x, –o로 끝나는 동사들은 동사 뒤에 ______________를 붙여요.
(fixes, washes, goes)

4 예외적으로 일반동사 have의 3인칭 단수형은 ______________예요.

Grammar Review Answer 정답

be동사의 부정문

1 be동사의 부정문은 be동사의 ___뒤___에 ___not___을 넣어서 만들 수 있어요.

2

주어	be동사	부정형	줄임말
I	am	am not	X
He / She / It	is	is not	's not / ___isn't___
We / You / They	are	are not	're not / ___aren't___

3 I am not의 am not은 줄일 수 ___없어요___.

일반동사의 부정문

1 일반동사의 부정문을 만들 때 주어가 I, You, 복수형이면 일반동사의 ___앞___에 ___do not___을 넣어서 만들어요.

2 그러나 주어가 3인칭 단수일 때는 일반동사의 ___앞___에 ___does not___을 넣어서 부정문을 만들어요.

3 부정문에서 do not이나 does not 뒤의 일반동사는 ___동사원형___이 와요.

4 do not은 ___don't___로 줄여 쓸 수 있어요.

5 does not은 ___doesn't___로 줄여 쓸 수 있어요.

의문사로 의문문 만들기

1 6개의 의문사에는 ___who___(누가), ___when___(언제), ___where___(어디서), ___what___(무엇을), ___how___(어떻게), ___why___(왜)가 있어요.

2 의문사를 이용해 의문문을 만들 때에는 be동사 의문문 또는 일반동사 의문문의 ___문장 맨 앞___에 의문사를 붙어주면 돼요.

일반동사의 3인칭 단수형

1 일반동사의 3인칭 단수형을 만들 때 대부분은 동사 뒤에 ___-s___를 붙여요.

2 동사가 「자음+y」로 끝나면 y를 ___i___로 고치고 ___-es___를 붙여요. (cries, studies, tries)

3 –s, –sh, –ch, –x, –o로 끝나는 동사들은 동사 뒤에 ___-es___를 붙여요. (fixes, washes, goes)

4 예외적으로 일반동사 have의 3인칭 단수형은 ___has___예요.

정답은 뒷면에서 확인하세요.

Unscramble and write.

순서에 맞게 단어를 써 보세요.

1.

r b i

rib

2.

i k d

3.

p i g

4.

w n i

5.

i b b

6.

l i d

7.

b g i

8.

i p n

Unscramble and write.

순서에 맞게 단어를 써 보세요.

1.

b r i

rib

2.

k i d

kid

3.

i p g

pig

4.

n w i

win

5.

b i b

bib

6.

i l d

lid

7.

g b i

big

8.

p i n

pin

MOTHERTONGUE
마더텅출판사
since1999.4.1.

초등영문법 3800제

정답과 해설

입문 2단계 일반동사, be동사의 부정문과 의문문 / 의문사 의문문

LEVEL 2

초등영문법
3800제
정답과 해설

2
LEVEL

입문 2단계

Chapter 01 일반동사

Unit 01 일반동사의 종류

Check and Write
▶ 본문 p.9

2. want　3. play　4. like　5. go

Unit 02 일반동사의 현재형

Check and Write
▶ 본문 p.11

2. have　3. wakes up　4. cook
5. live　6. eat

Practice 1
▶ 본문 p.12

A　2. get up　3. put on　4. eat
　5. brush　6. walk
B　1. likes　2. stays up　3. listens
　4. sleeps　5. has　6. wakes
C　1. wake up　2. sleep　3. go
　4. hate　5. want
D　1. study　2. have　3. keep

Practice 2
▶ 본문 p.14

2. I keep my fingers crossed
내가 행운을 빌게.
3. He does his homework
4. I play video games
5. I have an English test
6. I play soccer
7. I have the flu
나 독감 걸렸어.
8. I have a runny nose
나 콧물 나와.
9. I hate shots
나는 주사가 싫어!
10. I have a fever
11. She nags me
그녀는 나에게 잔소리를 해.
12. I watch "Crayon Shin-chan"
나는 '짱구는 못 말려'를 봐.
13. You use your smartphone
14. They fall down and get up again
그들은 넘어지고 다시 일어나는 거야.
15. I like warm hugs
난 따뜻한 포옹을 좋아해.
16. We read many books
우리는 책을 많이 읽어.
17. They eat ice cream
그들은 아이스크림을 먹는다.
18. Old habits die hard
오래된 습관은 고치기 어렵다. (세 살 버릇 여든까지 간다.)
19. I have no special talents
나는 특별한 재능들을 가지고 있지 않다.
20. I destroy my enemies

Practice 3
▶ 본문 p.17

2. I dislike "Pororo"
나는 '뽀로로'를 싫어해.
3. I want a bicycle
4. I need a break
난 휴식이 필요해.
5. Many kids watch cartoons
6. I sleep until 11 o'clock
7. I want a "One Piece" figure
8. I watch "Gag Concert" on Sundays
나는 일요일에 '개그콘서트'를 본다.
9. Most kids go to bed early on Sundays
대부분의 아이들은 일요일에 일찍 잔다.
10. I hate Mondays
나는 월요일이 싫어!
11. We hate Mondays
우리는 월요일을 싫어한다.
12. We do our homework
우리는 우리의 숙제를 한다.
13. I get up late and go to school in a hurry
나는 늦게 일어나서 서둘러 학교에 간다.
14. My mom[mother] nags me
나의 엄마는 나에게 잔소리를 하신다.
15. They play soccer
16. You swim well
너는 수영을 잘한다.
17. Mina loves you
미나가 너를 사랑해.
18. I have no special talents
나는 특별한 재능들을 가지고 있지 않다.
19. I keep my smartphone at home
나는 집에서 나의 스마트폰을 달고 산다.
20. I like Sihu
나는 시후가 좋아.

Let's Practice More!

SET 01
▶ 본문 p.20

02. ×　03. ○　04. ×　05. ○
06. ×　07. ○　08. ○　09. ×
10. ×　11. ○　12. ○

SET 02
▶ 본문 p.21

02. speak　03. have　04. put on　05. are
06. study　07. live　08. is　09. likes
10. brush　11. likes　12. want　13. have
14. is

SET 03
▶ 본문 p.22

02. wakes　03. speak　04. are　05. have
06. have　07. is　08. teach　09. die
10. is　11. want　12. do　13. eat
14. likes

SET 04

▶ 본문 p.23

02. ×	03. ×	04. ○	05. ×
06. ○	07. ○	08. ×	09. ○
10. ○	11. ×	12. ○	13. ×
14. ×			

SET 05

▶ 본문 p.24

02. brush	03. stays	04. make	05. has
06. go	07. keep	08. live	09. use
10. read	11. loves	12. need	

SET 06

▶ 본문 p.25

02. speak	03. wakes	04. go	05. keep
06. swim	07. go	08. want	09. has
10. rises	11. sleep	12. eat	13. like
14. nags			

SET 07

▶ 본문 p.26

02. have	03. wakes	04. make	05. play
06. likes	07. stays	08. study	09. have
10. teach	11. like	12. read	13. loves
14. watch	15. swim	16. do	17. eat
18. get	19. plays	20. has	

SET 08

▶ 본문 p.28

02. She puts on her glasses
그녀는 그녀의 안경을 쓴다.

03. I listen to Exo's music
나는 엑소의 음악을 듣는다.

04. They want a vacation
그들은 방학을 원해!

05. He speaks English very well
그는 영어를 아주 잘 해.

06. He has an English test next Monday
그는 다음 주 월요일에 영어시험을 봐.

07. I do my homework after school
나는 방과 후에 나의 숙제를 한다.

08. We play computer games
우리는 컴퓨터 게임을 한다.

09. She goes to the movies every Saturday
그녀는 토요일마다 영화를 보러 가.

10. Mina keeps her smartphone at home
미나는 집에서 스마트폰을 달고 산다.

11. He eats breakfast with his family
그는 가족들과 아침을 먹는다.

12. They have a math test this Thursday
그들은 이번 주 목요일에 수학시험을 쳐.

13. My mom always nags me
우리 엄마는 항상 내게 잔소리를 한다.

14. We need your help
우리는 너의 도움이 필요해.

15. Mom dislikes "Pororo"
엄마는 '뽀로로'를 싫어해.

16. You go to school in a hurry
너는 서둘러 학교에 간다.

17. She likes Sihu
그녀는 시후를 좋아해.

18. I have sweet dreams every night
나는 매일 밤 좋은 꿈을 꾼다.

19. We walk to school at eight
우리는 8시에 걸어서 학교에 간다.

20. Mom, she has a fever
엄마, 그녀는 열나요.

Unit 03 일반동사의 3인칭 단수형 (1)

Check and Write

▶ 본문 p.31

2. wants	3. eats	4. runs	5. drives

Unit 04 일반동사의 3인칭 단수형 (2)

Check and Write

▶ 본문 p.33

2. goes	3. cries	4. teaches	5. has

Practice 1

▶ 본문 p.34

A	2. opens	3. takes out	4. washes	5. cut
	6. make	7. cleans	8. puts	9. says
B	1. works	2. teaches	3. goes	4. studies
	5. plays	6. loves	7. watches	8. likes
C	1. drives	2. rides	3. takes	4. walks

Practice 2

▶ 본문 p.36

2. My dog kisses me
나의 개는 나에게 뽀뽀를 해.

3. He solves the problem
그는 문제를 해결해.

4. Junsu wants Nintendo
준수는 닌텐도를 원해요.

5. Sihu plays board games
시후는 보드게임을 한다.

6. He likes playing board games
그는 보드게임 하는 것을 좋아한다.

7. My teacher teaches math
나의 선생님은 수학을 가르치셔.

8. Sihu does his homework

9. Nayeon plays board games
나연이는 보드게임을 해.

10. I play board games

11. Mom scolds me
엄마는 나를 혼내셔.

12. something bad always happens

13. Your voice sounds so odd
목소리가 너무 이상하게 들려요.

14. A stitch in time saves nine
제때의 바느질 한 번이 아홉 번의 바느질을 던다.

15. The early bird catches the worm
일찍 일어나는 새가 벌레를 잡는다.

16. The world has so many lessons
세상은 아주 많은 교훈을 가지고 있다.

Practice 3

▶ 본문 p.38

2. A mailman delivers letters
우체부는 편지를 배달해요.

3. My mother washes the vegetables
나의 엄마는 야채를 씻어요.

4. I cut the onions

나는 양파를 썰어요.

5. Every puzzle has an answer
모든 퍼즐은 해답을 가지고 있어요.
6. A firefighter wears an orange uniform
소방관은 주황색 유니폼을 입어요.
7. Mina sends a letter
미나는 편지를 보내요.
8. Sihu writes a letter to Mina
시후는 미나에게 편지를 써요.
9. My homeroom teacher teaches English
나의 담임 선생님은 영어를 가르치세요.
10. A panda eats bamboo leaves
판다가 대나무 잎을 먹어요.
11. My grandpa reads books
나의 할아버지는 책을 읽어요.
12. Mina dislikes going to the dentist
미나는 치과에 가는 것을 싫어해요.
13. She brushes her teeth three times a day
그녀는 하루에 세 번 양치를 해요.
14. She says hello to the students
그녀는 학생들에게 인사를 해요.
15. He has a good voice
그는 좋은 목소리를 가지고 있어요.
16. Mina drinks milk for breakfast
미나는 아침으로 우유를 마셔요.
17. Bakers bake bread
제빵사들은 빵을 구워요.
18. Mina loves bread
미나는 빵을 아주 좋아해요.
19. My younger brother copies pandas
내 남동생은 판다를 따라 해요.

Let's Practice More!

SET 01
▶ 본문 p.40

02. ○	03. ×	04. ○	05. ×
06. ○	07. ○	08. ○	09. ×
10. ×	11. ○	12. ×	

SET 02
▶ 본문 p.41

02. studies	03. sounds	04. catches	05. brushes
06. copies	07. delivers	08. watches	09. bakes
10. happens	11. tries	12. relaxes	

SET 03
▶ 본문 p.42

02. does	03. studies	04. plays	05. tries
06. watches	07. sounds	08. walks	09. teaches
10. says	11. brushes	12. drinks	13. wants
14. helps			

SET 04
▶ 본문 p.43

02. ×	03. ○	04. ×	05. ×
06. ○	07. ×	08. ○	09. ×
10. ○	11. ×	12. ○	

SET 05
▶ 본문 p.44

02. saves	03. begins	04. wake	05. wear
06. sends	07. eats	08. reads	09. dislikes
10. brush	11. teaches	12. say	13. has
14. play			

SET 06
▶ 본문 p.45

02. plays	03. solves	04. works	05. teaches
06. goes	07. studies	08. plays	09. loves
10. watches	11. likes	12. drives	13. rides
14. takes			

SET 07
▶ 본문 p.46

02. delivers	03. makes	04. opens	05. takes
06. washes	07. cuts	08. cleans	09. puts
10. says	11. scolds	12. has	13. sounds
14. saves	15. catches	16. plays	17. saves
18. begins	19. wakes	20. happens	

SET 08
▶ 본문 p.48

02. My grandfather reads books
우리 할아버지는 책을 읽으신다.
03. Mina drinks milk for breakfast
미나는 아침으로 우유를 마신다.
04. He bakes bread
그는 빵을 굽는다.
05. She loves bread
그녀는 빵을 아주 좋아한다.
06. My younger brother copies pandas
내 남동생은 판다를 따라 한다.
07. She prepares for the class
그녀는 수업을 준비한다.
08. My dad relaxes on weekends
우리 아빠는 주말에 휴식을 취하신다.
09. Sihu writes a letter to her
시후는 그녀에게 편지를 쓴다.
10. My mom helps me
우리 엄마는 나를 도와주신다.
11. She tries her best
그녀는 최선을 다한다.
12. Jane wants a doll
Jane은 인형을 원한다.
13. My grandma watches TV all day
나의 할머니는 하루 종일 TV를 보신다.
14. Mina sends a letter
미나는 편지를 보낸다.
15. A panda eats bamboo leaves
판다는 대나무 잎을 먹는다.
16. He dislikes going to the dentist
그는 치과에 가는 것을 싫어한다.
17. My homeroom teacher teaches English
우리 담임 선생님은 영어를 가르치신다.
18. The world has many lessons
세상은 많은 교훈을 가지고 있다.
19. My brother has a good voice
나의 남자 형제는 좋은 목소리를 가지고 있다.
20. She scolds him
그녀는 그를 혼낸다.

Chapter 02 be동사의 부정문과 의문문

Unit 01 be동사의 부정문

Check and Write
▶ 본문 p.53

2. am not
3. are not, aren't
4. is not, isn't
5. are not, aren't
6. is not, isn't

Unit 02 be동사의 의문문

Check and Write
▶ 본문 p.55

2. Are, am, I'm, not
3. Is, is, isn't
4. Is, is, isn't

Practice 1
▶ 본문 p.56

A 2. is, not 3. Is 4. is, not 5. is, not
6. Is 7. is 8. Are 9. are, not

B 1. is, not 2. Is 3. is, not 4. Is
5. is 6. is, not 7. is, not

C 1. Is 2. is, not 3. Is 4. is, not

Practice 2
▶ 본문 p.58

2. Are your parents strict
너의 부모님은 엄격하시니?
3. Is your father a good singer
너의 아버지는 노래를 잘 부르시니?
4. Is your grandparents' house
5. My brother is not smart
우리 형은 똑똑하지 않아.
6. Is Hayul a picky eater
하율이는 편식 하니? (입맛이 까다롭니?)
7. Hayul is not a grown-up
하율이는 어른이 아니야.
8. I am not happy
나는 행복하지 않다.
9. He is not a child
10. Are you tired
너는 피곤하니?
11. I am not a big eater
나는 대식가가 아니야.
12. My mother is not inside the house
우리 엄마는 집 안에 안 계세요.
13. Happiness is not far away
행복은 멀리 있지 않아.
14. They are not young
그들은 어리지 않아.
15. They are not your real friends
그들은 너의 진정한 친구들이 아니야.
16. I'm not your enemy
나는 너의 적이 아니다.
17. You are not weak
너는 약하지 않아.
18. Are you sad
너 슬프니?
19. Are you sure
확실해요?

Practice 3
▶ 본문 p.60

2. I am not[I'm not] lazy
난 게으르지 않아.
3. It is not[It isn't/It's not] easy
그것은 쉽지 않아.
4. Are you thirsty
너 목마르니?
5. Are you late for school
너는 학교에 늦니?
6. Are you hungry
너희들은 배가 고프니?
7. No, we are not[we aren't/we're not] hungry
아니, 우리는 배고프지 않아.
8. Sehun is not[Sehun isn't] a good rapper
세훈이는 랩을 잘 하지 못한다.
9. Are you a good rapper
너는 랩을 잘 하니?
10. I am not[I'm not] a good rapper
나는 랩을 못 해.
11. Is he your best friend
그는 너의 가장 친한 친구니?
12. No, he is not[he isn't/he's not] my best friend
아니, 그는 내 가장 친한 친구가 아니야.
13. We are not[We aren't/We're not] in the same class
우리는 같은 반이 아니다.
14. Our classroom is not[Our classroom isn't] clean
우리 교실은 깨끗하지 않다.
15. Is the problem important
그 문제가 중요하니?
16. Is the webtoon funny
그 웹툰 재미있니?
17. The webtoon is not[The webtoon isn't] funny
그 웹툰은 재미없어.

Let's Practice More!

SET 01
▶ 본문 p.62

02. × 03. × 04. × 05. ○
06. ○ 07. × 08. ○ 09. ×
10. ○ 11. ○ 12. ×

SET 02
▶ 본문 p.63

02. is not 03. is not 04. is not 05. are not
06. am not 07. is not 08. are not 09. is not
10. is not 11. are not 12. is not 13. are not
14. is not

SET 03
▶ 본문 p.64

02. I'm not 03. isn't 04. isn't 05. isn't
06. aren't 07. isn't 08. isn't 09. aren't
10. aren't 11. isn't 12. I'm not 13. aren't
14. aren't

SET 04

▶ 본문 p.65

02. Is 03. Is 04. Is 05. Are
06. Is 07. Am 08. Are 09. Is
10. Are 11. Are 12. Is

SET 05

▶ 본문 p.66

02. Is she angry
그녀는 화났니?
03. Is she a good singer
그녀는 노래를 잘 부르니?
04. Is their house in the city
그들의 집은 도시에 있니?
05. Is the webtoon funny
그 웹툰은 재미있니?
06. Are you hungry
너는 배고프니?
07. Are they your friends
그들은 너의 친구들이니?
08. Is he a teacher
그는 선생님이니?
09. Is the problem important
그 문제는 중요하니?
10. Is he a baseball player
그는 야구 선수이니?
11. Is Mike a picky eater
Mike는 입맛이 까다로운 사람이니?
12. Are you late for school
너는 학교에 늦었니?
13. Am I lazy
나는 게으르니?
14. Are they young
그들은 어리니?

SET 06

▶ 본문 p.68

02. it is, it is not[it isn't/it's not]
03. I am, I am not[I'm not]
04. she is, she is not[she isn't/she's not]
05. I am, I am not[I'm not]
06. it is, it is not[it isn't/it's not]
07. we are, we are not[we aren't/we're not]
08. they are, they are not[they aren't/they're not]
09. he is, he is not[he isn't/he's not]
10. she is, she is not[she isn't/she's not]
11. he is, he is not[he isn't/he's not]
12. I am, I am not[I'm not]
13. they are, they are not[they aren't/they're not]
14. she is, she is not[she isn't/she's not]

SET 07

▶ 본문 p.70

02. The baby is not[isn't] awake
그 아기는 깨어있지 않아.
03. Your dog is not[isn't] cute
너의 개는 귀엽지 않아.
04. She is not[She isn't/She's not] rich
그녀는 부유하지 않아.
05. Hayul is not[isn't] a big eater
하율이는 대식가가 아니야.
06. My father is not[isn't] a good singer
나의 아빠는 노래를 잘 못 부르셔.
07. Irene is not[isn't] a smart girl
Irene은 똑똑한 소녀가 아니야.
08. We are not[We aren't/We're not] sleepy
우리는 졸리지 않아.
09. I am not[I'm not] a fool
나는 바보가 아니야.
10. My mom is not[isn't] inside the house
나의 엄마는 집 안에 계시지 않아.
11. They are not[They aren't/They're not] tired
그들은 피곤하지 않아.
12. You are not[You aren't/You're not] weak
너는 약하지 않아.
13. The problem is not[isn't] important
그 문제는 중요하지 않아.
14. Our classroom is not[isn't] clean
우리의 교실은 깨끗하지 않아.
15. The webtoon is not[isn't] funny
그 웹툰은 재미있지 않아.
16. They are not[They aren't/They're not] your real friends
그들은 너의 진정한 친구들이 아니야.
17. She is not[She isn't/She's not] afraid of birds
그녀는 새를 두려워하지 않아.
18. We are not[We aren't/We're not] in the same class
우리는 같은 반이 아니야.
19. My parents are not[aren't] in Seoul
나의 부모님은 서울에 계시지 않아.
20. I am not[I'm not] lazy
나는 게으르지 않아.

SET 08

▶ 본문 p.72

02. are, not 03. is, not 04. are, not
05. Are, you 06. Is, your 07. is, not
08. am, not 09. Is, he 10. are, not
11. is, not 12. Are, they 13. is, not
14. Are, you 15. Is, she 16. Are, they
17. am, not 18. is, not 19. is, not
20. Are, you

Chapter 01~02 실전테스트

▶ 본문 p.74

01. is, not 02. ④ 03. ① 04. ③
05. ③ 06. ④ 07. ④
08. A cat eats ice cream. 고양이가 아이스크림을 먹는다.
09. The princess is pretty. 공주는 예쁘다.
10. I love animals. 나는 동물들을 사랑한다.
11. Jenny likes red shoes. Jenny는 빨간 구두를 좋아한다.
12. They dance at school. 그들은 학교에서 춤을 춘다.
13. Are you from China? 너는 중국에서 왔니?
14. She is not angry. 그녀는 화나지 않았다.
15. reads 16. carries 17. is 18. ④
19. plays 20. look 21. like 22. plays
23. goes 24. ② 25. ② 26. Is, she is
27. She has breakfast every day. 그녀는 매일 아침을 먹는다.
28. It is your cat. 그것은 너의 고양이이다.
29. We like you. 우리는 너를 좋아한다.
30. Tom eats bread. Tom은 빵을 먹는다.

Chapter 03 일반동사의 부정문과 의문문

Unit 01 일반동사의 부정문

Check and Write

▶ 본문 p.81

2. does not, doesn't 3. do not, don't
4. do not, don't 5. does not, doesn't

Unit 02 일반동사의 의문문

Check and Write

▶ 본문 p.83

2. Does, does, doesn't 3. Do, do, don't
4. Does, does, doesn't 5. Do, do, don't

Practice 1

▶ 본문 p.84

A 2. Does, does 3. Does, does 4. Do, don't
5. Does, doesn't

B 1. Do, do 2. Do, do 3. Does, doesn't
4. Do, do

C 1. Do, don't 2. Do, don't 3. Do, don't
4. Do, do

D 1. don't 2. don't 3. doesn't
4. don't 5. don't 6. Do
7. doesn't

Practice 2

▶ 본문 p.87

2. Do you eat fish
너희는 생선을 먹니?
3. People don't like the movie
4. Do students like club activities
학생들은 동아리 활동을 좋아하니?
5. Does your dog jump high
너의 개는 높이 점프하니?
6. Do we have an English test
7. Do you take a walk
8. I don't have time
나는 시간이 없다.
9. doesn't like bananas
10. Does Jane study with Karen
Jane은 Karen과 함께 공부하니?
11. I don't wear a muffler
12. He doesn't care about
13. I don't remember Karen's birthday
나는 Karen의 생일이 기억나지 않는다.
14. Students don't take notes
15. They don't go
16. Do your parents come
17. Do I play games
18. Do you like the color blue
너는 파란색을 좋아하니?
19. Do your friends play baseball

Practice 3

▶ 본문 p.90

2. Do your friends go to the library
너의 친구들은 도서관에 가니?
3. I don't eat breakfast
나는 아침밥을 먹지 않는다.
4. Sam doesn't care about
5. I don't remember his phone number
나는 그의 전화번호가 기억나지 않는다.
6. Students don't listen to their teacher
학생들은 선생님의 말을 듣지 않는다.
7. Mina doesn't like
8. Children don't like sad movies
아이들은 슬픈 영화를 좋아하지 않는다.
9. Does your computer make noise
너의 컴퓨터는 소음을 내니?
10. Do turtles swim fast
거북이가 빨리 헤엄치니?
11. Do you eat beans
너는 콩을 먹니?
12. I don't wear a watch
나는 손목시계를 차지 않는다.
13. Do we have a math class
14. Does your sister share clothes
15. I don't like movies
나는 영화를 좋아하지 않는다.
16. They don't go to church
그들은 교회에 가지 않는다.
17. Do you like the color violet
너는 보라색을 좋아하니?
18. Do your friends eat snacks
19. Does Jane like jelly
Jane은 젤리를 좋아하니?

Let's Practice More!

SET 01

▶ 본문 p.92

02. × 03. × 04. ○ 05. ○
06. ○ 07. × 08. × 09. ×
10. ○ 11. ○ 12. ×

SET 02

▶ 본문 p.93

02. do not 03. does not 04. do not
05. do not 06. do not 07. do not
08. does not 09. do not 10. does not
11. do not 12. does not 13. do not
14. does not

SET 03

▶ 본문 p.94

02. doesn't 03. don't 04. don't 05. ○
06. ○ 07. don't 08. ○ 09. ○
10. don't 11. doesn't 12. doesn't 13. ○
14. doesn't

SET 04

▶ 본문 p.95

02. Does 03. Do 04. Does 05. Do
06. Do 07. Do 08. Does 09. Do
10. Does 11. Does 12. Do 13. Does
14. Does

SET 05

▶ 본문 p.96

02. Does your father play badminton
너의 아버지는 배드민턴을 치시니?
03. Do pigeons walk fast
비둘기는 빨리 걷니?
04. Do your parents come to school
너의 부모님은 학교에 오시니?
05. Do your friends play baseball
너의 친구들은 야구하니?
06. Do people like the movie, "Batman vs. Superman"
사람들은 영화 '배트맨 대 슈퍼맨'을 좋아하니?
07. Do you drink a lot of water
너 물 많이 마시니?
08. Does your dog jump high
너의 개는 높이 점프하니?
09. Does Jack study with Ben
Jack은 Ben과 함께 공부하니?
10. Do your friends play soccer after school
너의 친구들은 방과 후에 축구를 하니?
11. Does Mina like action movies
미나는 액션 영화를 좋아하니?
12. Do turtles swim fast
거북이가 빨리 헤엄치니?
13. Does your computer make noise
너의 컴퓨터는 소음을 내니?
14. Do we have a math class today
오늘 우리 수학 수업이 있니?

SET 06

▶ 본문 p.98

02. he does, he doesn't
03. we do, we don't
04. I[we] do, I[we] don't
05. he does, he doesn't
06. I[we] do, I[we] don't
07. I[we] do, I[we] don't
08. he does, he doesn't
09. she does, she doesn't
10. they do, they don't
11. they do, they don't
12. she does, she doesn't
13. I[we] do, I[we] don't
14. you do, you don't

SET 07

▶ 본문 p.100

02. You don't eat fish
너는 생선을 먹지 않는다.
03. Your parents don't come to school
너의 부모님은 학교에 오시지 않는다.
04. Do students like the lunch menu
학생들이 점심 메뉴를 좋아하니?
05. Do your friends go to the cyber cafe
너의 친구들은 PC방에 가니?
06. Do your friends play baseball
너의 친구들은 야구하니?
07. Does he care about other people
그는 다른 사람들에 대해 신경 쓰니?
08. Jake doesn't fight with Mark every day
Jake는 Mark와 매일 싸우지 않는다.
09. Do you go to the library
너는 도서관에 가니?
10. You don't want some juice
너는 주스를 원하지 않는다.
11. Do they take pictures
그들은 사진을 찍니?
12. Students don't like club activities
학생들은 동아리 활동을 좋아하지 않는다.
13. Does your dog jump high
너의 개는 높이 점프하니?
14. Does Mina like action movies
미나는 액션 영화를 좋아하니?
15. Do ducks walk fast
오리가 빨리 걷니?
16. Your computer doesn't make noise
너의 컴퓨터는 소음을 내지 않는다.
17. Does Jane like jelly
Jane은 젤리를 좋아하니?
18. Do we have an English test today
우리 오늘 영어 시험을 보니?
19. Does Sam care about his health
Sam은 그의 건강에 대해 신경 쓰니?
20. You don't take a walk with your dog
너는 너의 개와 함께 산책을 하지 않는다.

SET 08

▶ 본문 p.102

02. does, not
03. Do
04. do, not
05. do, not
06. Do
07. Does
08. don't
09. doesn't
10. Does
11. don't
12. don't
13. does, not
14. Do
15. do, not
16. don't
17. doesn't
18. does, not
19. don't
20. don't

Chapter 04 의문사 의문문

Unit 01 의문사가 있는 의문문 만드는 법

Check and Write

▶ 본문 p.107

2. When do you leave
너는 언제 떠나니?
3. What is your favorite food
네가 가장 좋아하는 음식은 무엇이니?
4. Who do you meet
너는 누구를 만나니?
5. Where do you go
너는 어디에 가니?

Unit 02 who/what 의문문

Check and Write
▶ 본문 p.109

2. What 3. Who 4. What 5. Who
6. What

Practice 1
▶ 본문 p.110

A 2. What 3. What 4. Who 5. Who
B 1. What 2. Who 3. is 4. are
5. does
C 1. do 2. Who 3. is 4. Who
5. What
D 1. is 2. says 3. wakes 4. does
5. do

Practice 2
▶ 본문 p.112

2. What is her name
그녀의 이름은 무엇이니?
3. Who is that woman
저 여자 분은 누구니?
4. What is that
5. Who are those people
저 사람들은 누구니?
6. What do you want
넌 무엇을 원해?
7. What do I do
8. What is wrong
9. Who is that girl
10. Who teases Mina
누가 미나를 놀리니?
11. What is Sihu's phone number
시후의 전화번호는 뭐야?
12. What do they do
13. What is going on
14. What do people eat
사람들은 뭘 먹니?
15. What is this place
이 장소는 무엇인가요?
16. Who is your homeroom teacher
너의 담임선생님은 누구니?
17. Who says
18. Who are you
넌 누구니?
19. What is the key

Practice 3
▶ 본문 p.115

2. Who is your best friend
너의 제일 친한 친구는 누구니?
3. What does he read
그는 무엇을 읽나요?
4. Who is angry
누가 화났니?
5. What do you want
6. Who does he help
그는 누구를 돕니?
7. What does he bring
그는 무엇을 가져오니?
8. What do you do
9. Who reads a book
누가 책을 읽니?
10. Who does he like
그는 누구를 좋아하니?
11. What is your job
당신의 직업은 무엇인가요?
12. What does she do
13. What do you need
너는 무엇이 필요하니?
14. Who do you meet
너는 누구를 만나니?
15. What are your plans
16. Who do you visit
17. What is your hobby
너의 취미는 뭐니?
18. What do we eat
19. Who cleans the bathroom
누가 화장실을 청소하니?
20. What does Mina buy
미나는 무엇을 사니?

Let's Practice More!

SET 01
▶ 본문 p.118

02. What 03. Who 04. What 05. Who
06. What 07. What 08. Who 09. What
10. What 11. Who 12. What

SET 02
▶ 본문 p.119

02. Who is that little boy
저 작은 남자아이는 누구니?
03. What is that smell
저 냄새 뭐야?(무슨 냄새야?)
04. What is that on your desk
네 책상 위에 있는 저것은 무엇이니?
05. Who are those people
저 사람들은 누구야?
06. What is your favorite game
네가 가장 좋아하는 게임은 무엇이니?
07. What are you doing now
넌 지금 무엇을 하고 있니?
08. What is Sihu's phone number
시후의 전화번호는 무엇이니?
09. What are your plans for vacation
너의 방학 계획은 무엇이니?
10. Who is your brother
누가 너의 오빠이니?
11. What is your problem
너의 문제는 무엇이니?
12. What is the key to happiness
행복의 열쇠는 무엇이니?

SET 03
▶ 본문 p.120

02. likes 03. do 04. do 05. does
06. ○ 07. do 08. ○ 09. does
10. do 11. do 12. ○ 13. ○
14. does

SET 04

▶ 본문 p.121

02. does he	03. do you	04. does he
05. do you	06. do people	07. does she
08. do you	09. does he	10. do they
11. does he	12. do you do	13. do you
14. do you		

SET 05

▶ 본문 p.122

02. Who	03. Who	04. What	05. What
06. Who	07. What	08. What	09. What
10. Who	11. Who	12. What	13. Who
14. What			

SET 06

▶ 본문 p.123

02. Who	03. What	04. Who	05. Who
06. What	07. Who	08. What	09. What
10. What	11. Who	12. What	

SET 07

▶ 본문 p.124

02. What, does	03. Who, is	04. What, do
05. Who, skips	06. What, is	07. Who, is
08. Who, does	09. What, is	10. Who, do
11. What, do	12. Who, is	13. What, does
14. What, are	15. Who, does	16. What, does
17. What, do	18. What, are	19. What, is
20. Who, teases		

SET 08

▶ 본문 p.126

02. What do they do on their birthday
그들은 그들의 생일에 무엇을 하니?

03. What is her name
그녀의 이름은 무엇이니?

04. Who wakes you up
누가 너를 깨워줘?

05. Who does he like
그는 누구를 좋아하니?

06. What is Sihu's phone number
시후의 전화번호는 뭐야?

07. Who helps me
누가 나를 도와줄 거야?

08. What do we eat for breakfast
우리는 아침으로 무엇을 먹어요?

09. Who is your homeroom teacher
너의 담임선생님은 누구니?

10. What is this place
이 장소는 무엇인가요?

11. What does Mina buy
미나가 무엇을 사니?

12. Who cleans the bathroom
누가 화장실을 청소하니?

13. What is the key to happiness
행복의 열쇠는 무엇이니?

14. Who is your best friend
너의 제일 친한 친구는 누구니?

15. Who is angry
누가 화났니?

16. What do you want for your birthday
너는 생일 선물로 무엇을 원하니?

17. Who are those people
저 사람들은 누구니?

18. What is your hobby
넌 취미가 뭐니?

19. What do you do for your friend
너의 친구를 위해 너는 무엇을 해?

20. Who reads a book
누가 책을 읽니?

Unit 03 when/where 의문문

Check and Write

▶ 본문 p.129

2. Where are you
너 어디에 있어?

3. Where do they play
그들은 어디에서 놀아?

4. When does he study
그는 언제 공부해?

5. Where do we go
우리 어디 가요?

Unit 04 how/why 의문문

Check and Write

▶ 본문 p.131

2. Why	3. Because	4. How	5. Why
6. Because			

Practice 1

▶ 본문 p.132

A	2. How	3. Where	4. When	
B	1. How	2. is	3. Why	4. Because
C	1. When	2. leave	3. How	4. go
	5. does	6. takes	7. do	8. arrive
	9. Why	10. Because	11. Where	12. play

Practice 2

▶ 본문 p.134

2. Where is my dog
내 개가 어디에 있지?

3. How are your parents
너희 부모님은 어떻게 지내시니? (너희 부모님은 안녕하시니?)

4. Where are you from
너는 어디에서 왔니? (너는 어디 출신이니?)

5. Where do you want to go
너는 어디에 가고 싶어?

6. Where do you find your dog
너는 어디에서 너의 개를 발견하니?

7. When does your girlfriend come
너의 여자친구는 언제 오니?

8. How is my hair
내 머리 어때요?

9. Why do you like her
넌 그녀가 왜 좋아?

10. Why are you happy
너 왜 행복해?

11. How are you
너는 어떻게 지내? (안녕?)

12. Why is dad so late
아빠는 왜 이렇게 늦어요?

13. Where do you live

너 어디에 살아?

14. When is your birthday
너의 생일은 언제니?

15. How do you know
네가 어떻게 아니?

16. Why do you want

17. How do I look
나 어때 보여?

18. Why do you buy a cake
너는 왜 케이크를 사니?

19. How much is it
그것은 얼마니?

20. Why are you busy
너는 왜 바빠?

Practice 3

▶ 본문 p.137

2. Why do you blame me
왜 저를 탓하세요?

3. How is the weather
날씨 어때?

4. How do I look
나 어때 보여?

5. How do you feel
너는 기분이 어떠니?

6. When do I pick you up
내가 언제 너를 데리러 갈까?

7. How do you know Mina
네가 미나를 어떻게 알아?

8. Where do you study
넌 어디에서 공부하니?

9. How does he arrive

10. When do you do your homework
너는 언제 숙제를 해?

11. Why do you follow me
너 왜 나 따라와?

12. How do you know each other
너희들은 서로 어떻게 알아?

13. Where do we meet
우리 어디서 만나?

14. When do we meet
우리 언제 만나지?

15. When do you wake up
너는 언제 일어나니?

16. Where does the dog sleep
그 개는 어디서 자니?

17. Where is the bookstore
서점은 어디 있니?

18. When does the store open
그 상점은 언제 열어?

19. Why are you nice to me
너 나한테 왜 잘해줘?

20. Why is he great
왜 그가 훌륭해?

Let's Practice More!

SET 01

▶ 본문 p.140

02. How 03. When 04. How 05. How
06. Why 07. Where 08. When 09. Where
10. Where 11. How 12. Why

SET 02

▶ 본문 p.141

02. Why 03. When 04. ○ 05. ○
06. ○ 07. When 08. ○ 09. When
10. Why 11. ○ 12. When 13. ○
14. Why

SET 03

▶ 본문 p.142

02. ○ 03. × 04. ○ 05. ×
06. × 07. × 08. ○ 09. ×
10. × 11. ○ 12. ○ 13. ○
14. ×

SET 04

▶ 본문 p.143

02. How do 03. How is 04. How do
05. Where do 06. When do 07. Where does
08. When does 09. Why is 10. When did
11. Why do 12. When do

SET 05

▶ 본문 p.144

02. do 03. is 04. are 05. are
06. does 07. is 08. are 09. do
10. is 11. do 12. do 13. do
14. does

SET 06

▶ 본문 p.145

02. I, go 03. I, like, rain
04. school, at 05. takes, minutes
06. arrive, home 07. play, soccer
08. play, playground 09. arrive
10. Because, present 11. look, happy
12. meet, my, friend 13. Because, homework
14. are, classmates

SET 07

▶ 본문 p.147

02. How, do 03. How, much 04. Where, does
05. Where, do 06. Why, do 07. How, is
08. How, do 09. When, do 10. How, do
11. How, do 12. Where, do 13. When, do
14. Where, is 15. How, does 16. Why, are
17. Why, is 18. When, do 19. Where, is
20. When, does

SET 08

▶ 본문 p.148

02. Why are you
03. Why do you
04. When do you
05. How do you
06. Where do you play
너희들은 어디서 놀아?
07. How long
08. When do you
09. When do we
10. Where
11. Why do you
12. When do you
13. Why do you

14. When do you
15. Where is
16. When does
17. Why are you
18. Where are you from
너는 어디에서 왔니?(너는 어디 출신이니?)
19. Why do you like her
넌 그녀가 왜 좋아?
20. Why do you buy

Chapter 03~04 실전테스트

▶ 본문 p.150

01. ②
02. (1) is (2) is
03. (1) Does (2) does
04. ②
05. (H)ow, (d)o
06. When, does
07. ②
08. ④
09. Does he wear a coat? 그는 코트를 입니?
10. What do you see? 너는 무엇을 보니?
11. When, Do
12. (1) is (2) is
13. (1) Does (2) does
14. (1) Do (2) do
15. ①
16. I do not[don't] need a rest. 난 휴식이 필요 하지 않아.
17. She does not[doesn't] want to go there.
그녀는 그곳에 가고 싶지 않아 해.
18. Does he like running? 그는 달리는 것을 좋아하니?
19. Do you want a puppy? 너는 강아지 한 마리를 원하니?
20. ③
21. ②
22. ②
23. 축구 경기를 보러 간다.
24. She does not walk to school.
그녀는 학교로 걸어가지 않아.
25. Does he bake bread? 그는 빵을 굽니?
26. ④
27. ③
28. Does Mary like cats? Mary는 고양이를 좋아하니?
29. Do you study English? 너는 영어를 공부하니?
30. ①

초등영문법 3800제 서평

초등3학년 아이.. 원서는 어느 정도 잘 읽는데.. 글씨 쓰는 걸 많이 어려워해요. 그래서 문법을 알면 도움이 되지 않을까 싶어서 찾다가 3800제를 만났네요. 초등 저학년 아이가 혼자서 하는데 있어서 어려움이 없어요. 쉬운 단어로 설명을 해주니 쉽게 이해하고 공책에 배운 걸 써보기도 하면서 혼자서 열심히 공부하고 있어요. 2번, 3번 쭈욱~~ 3800제로 나갈까 합니다. ***YES24*** / 은**주

형이 중학교 진학 전부터 중학생용 3800제를 풀고 있었고 3800제 구성이 만족스러워서 초등 동생도 풀기 시작했어요. 개념도 구체적이고 다양한 내용이 있어서 좋았어요. 지루하지 않게 그림이 자주 삽입되어 있으니까 덜 삭막해요^^ 무엇보다 다각도로 연습문제가 진짜진짜 많아요. 어설프게 알고 진도 나가면 나중에 다시 봤을 때 까먹게 되고 제대로 이해 못하게 되거든요. 다양한 방식의 문제를 풀면서 영어실력이 확장되는 게 느껴져요. 게임, 마크만 성실, 꼼꼼하게 하지 공부는 대충 해치우고 마는 아이인데 이 교재를 통해서 언젠가는 영어 실력이 차곡차곡 쌓이길 기대해봅니다. 뒷편에는 단어 공부, 받아쓰기 연습을 할 수 있는 것도 있어요. 아이 핸드폰에 mp3파일을 넣어주면 스스로 할 수 있겠더라구요. 아직은 진도를 빨리 빼느라 숙제주진 않았는데 방학 시작하면 이 한권으로 영어공부는 충분할 것 같습니다. 핸드폰이 게임, 유튜브 보는 것만이 아닌 공부할 적에도 사용하는 것이라는 것을 알게 되길~^^; ***YES24*** / 희*

잠수네로 별칭되는 엄마표 영어를 한 지 몇 년 되었는데 엄마가 너무 띄엄띄엄 지도하다 보니 아이 단어와 문법이 많이 약한 것 같아 문법 교재로 구매했습니다. Unit 시작할 때 단어가 스물 몇 개 있고 의미를 인지하고 있는지 셀프 테스팅 하도록 구성되어 있고 개념 문제 뒤 연습문제가 쭉 있어서 아이가 스스로 정리하며 공부할 수 있어요. 난이도는 쉬운 편이라 차라리 부담 없이 스르륵 풀 수 있어서 좋아요. ***YES24*** / d**rh0424

문법은 실제로 문장 속에서 활용해봐야 이해가 쉽기 때문에 예제 중심의 반복학습이 가능한 책을 찾다가 선택한 교재입니다. 여러 형식으로 문제 풀이가 다양하게 제시되어 있어 문제를 풀다보면 그 원리가 절로 체득되어 정말 좋습니다. 아직 문법이라는 추상적인 개념을 이해하기 어려워하는 초등학생들에게 좋은 교재예요. 기존에 기초 문법의 틀이 조금 잡혀 있는 학생들은 자습용으로도 좋고 처음 문법을 접하는 학생들에게는 단계적으로 심화되는 문제 구성을 차근차근 밟아가며 공부하기에 좋습니다. ***YES24*** / a**owa

---

아이 문법 학습을 위해서 구입을 하게 되었습니다. 큰아이 중학영문법 3800제를 가지고 학습을 한 경험이 있어 믿고 구입하게 되었는데 역시나 초등문법도 많은 연습문제로 아이들이 같은 내용을 꾸준히 반복 연습하게 구성이 되어있어서 마음에 듭니다. 초등학생용이라 글씨도 큼직큼직하고 페이지마다 빈공간도 많이 있어 답답하지도 않아서 좋아요. 초등학생 아이들은 일단 글씨가 작고 빽빽하면 보면서 질려하는 경향이 있는데 이 교재는 그런 점에서는 후한 점수를 주고 싶네요. 단순 객관식 문제 풀이로 학습시키고 싶은 분들에게는 추천하지 않구요. 객관식 문제풀이가 단원 끝에 단원테스트에 조금 밖에 없어서요. 객관식 문제풀이가 아닌 아이가 문장을 만들면서 학습하기를 원하시는 분들에게는 강추합니다. 타 학습서들이 보통 초등문법을 2권 내지 3권에 끝내는 것을 이 초등영문법 3800제는 1권부터 8권까지에 연습할 부분을 나누어 놓았으니 얼마나 많은 반복을 시킬 수 있는지 권수만 봐도 알 수 있지요. 어쨌든, 초등학교 4학년 아이 8권까지 열심히 공부할 예정입니다. ***YES24*** / j**onim

book.toptutor.co.kr

구하기 어려운 교재는
마더텅 모바일(인터넷)을 이용하세요.
즉시 배송해 드립니다.

마더텅 학습 교재 이벤트에 참여해 주세요. 참여해 주신 모든 분께 선물을 드립니다.

이벤트 1 1분 간단 교재 사용 후기 이벤트

마더텅은 고객님의 소중한 의견을 반영하여 보다 좋은 책을 만들고자 합니다.
교재 구매 후, <교재 사용 후기 이벤트>에 **참여해 주신 모든 분**께는 감사의 마음을 담아 **모바일 문화상품권 1천 원권**을 보내 드립니다. 지금 바로 QR 코드를 스캔해 소중한 의견을 보내 주세요!

이벤트 2 학습계획표 이벤트

STEP 1 책을 다 풀고 SNS 또는 수험생 커뮤니티에 작성한 학습계획표 사진을 업로드

필수 태그 #마더텅 #초등영어 #초등영문법3800 #학습계획표 #공스타그램
SNS/수험생 커뮤니티 페이스북, 인스타그램, 블로그, 네이버/다음 카페 등

STEP 2 왼쪽 QR 코드를 스캔하여 작성한 게시물의 URL 인증

참여해 주신 모든 분께는 감사의 마음을 담아 **CU 모바일 편의점 상품권 1천 원권** 및 **B 북포인트 2천 점**을 드립니다.

이벤트 3 블로그/SNS 이벤트

STEP 1 자신의 블로그/SNS 중 하나에 마더텅 교재에 대한 사용 후기를 작성

필수 태그 #마더텅 #초등영어 #초등영문법3800 #교재리뷰 #공스타그램
필수 내용 마더텅 교재 장점, 교재 사진

STEP 2 왼쪽 QR 코드를 스캔하여 작성한 게시물의 URL 인증

참여해 주신 모든 분께는 감사의 마음을 담아 **CU 모바일 편의점 상품권 2천 원권** 및 **B 북포인트 3천 점**을 드립니다.
매달 우수 후기자를 선정하여 **모바일 문화상품권 2만 원권**과 **B 북포인트 1만 점**을 드립니다.

B 북포인트란? 마더텅 인터넷 서점 **http://book.toptutor.co.kr**에서 교재 구매 시 현금처럼 사용할 수 있는 포인트입니다.

※자세한 사항은 해당 QR 코드를 스캔하거나 홈페이지 이벤트 공지글을 참고해 주세요.
※당사 사정에 따라 이벤트의 내용이나 상품이 변경될 수 있으며 변경 시 홈페이지에 공지합니다. ※만 14세 미만은 부모님께서 신청해 주셔야 합니다.
※상품은 이벤트 참여일로부터 2~3일(영업일 기준) 내에 발송됩니다. ※동일 교재로 세 가지 이벤트 모두 참여 가능합니다. (단, 같은 이벤트 중복 참여는 불가합니다.)
※이벤트 기간: 2024년 12월 31일까지 (*해당 이벤트는 당사 사정에 따라 조기 종료될 수 있습니다.)

정답은 뒷면에서 확인하세요.

Look and write.

빠진 글자들을 써 보세요. 어떤 단어가 숨어 있을까요?

1.  

pan cake

2.  

do ______

3.  

______ tain

4.  

hic ______

Build up.

네모 안에 알맞은 알파벳을 쓰고 모아 보세요. 어떤 단어가 될까요?

1.  + 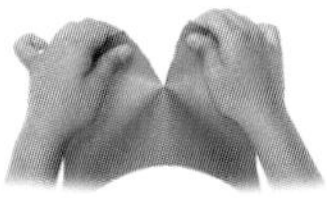 → 

[l]og + r[i][p] → [l][i][p]

2.  + 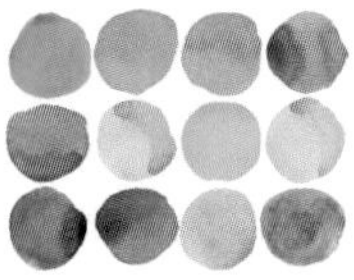 → 

[ ]an + d[ ][ ] → [ ][ ][ ]

3.  +  → 

[ ]ut + t[ ][ ] → [ ][ ][ ]

Look and write.

빠진 글자들을 써 보세요. 어떤 단어가 숨어 있을까요?

1.

pan cake

2.

do nut

3.

cap tain

4.

hic cup

Build up.

네모 안에 알맞은 알파벳을 쓰고 모아 보세요. 어떤 단어가 될까요?

1.

log

\+

rip

➡

lip

2.

pan

\+

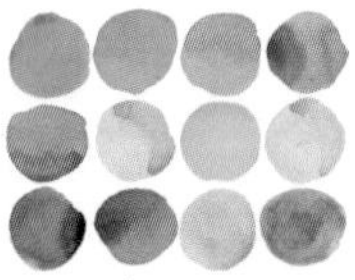

dot

➡

pot

3.

hut

\+

ten

➡

hen